# A SECOND OSWESTRY

aspects of
our local history

by
John Pryce-Jones

Llanforda Press
2020

**Front cover**: 'Fair Day on the Bailey Head, Oswestry' (1888), by George Frederick Bonner (1823-1896); reproduced courtesy of Oswestry Town Council.

BRITISH LIBRARY CATALOGUING IN PUBLICATION DATA
A catalogue record for this book is available from the British Library.

The moral right of the author has been asserted.

ISBN 978-0-9517162-5-0
© John Pryce-Jones, 2020
Printed by Walsall MBC Print and Design Service

# Contents

|  | Introduction and acknowledgements | Page 4 |
|---|---|---|
|  | Illustrations | Page 5 |
| 1. | Where exactly did king Oswald die? | Page 7 |
| 2. | Why Roft Street follows a crooked path – searching for St John's Hospital | Page 10 |
| 3. | Local evidence of the Black Death | Page 13 |
| 4. | Links to the court of king Henry VIII | Page 16 |
| 5 | Sickness and plague in Tudor and Stuart times | Page 20 |
| 6. | Eye witness tales of an attempted *coup* | Page 24 |
| 7. | An Elizabethan service contract | Page 30 |
| 8. | Looking back on Oswestry in the year 1611 | Page 33 |
| 9. | Edward Lloyd of Llwynymaen, a very difficult man | Page 36 |
| 10. | Hugh Yale and the Yale Monument | Page 39 |
| 11. | An investigation of Corporation malpractice | Page 45 |
| 12. | From Middleton to Aleppo – tales of a Turkey merchant | Page 47 |
| 13. | The importance of wool and leather to Oswestry's economy - evidence from the parish registers | Page 54 |
| 14. | Solving a mystery in the parish church | Page 59 |
| 15. | Playing host to the redcoats | Page 62 |
| 16. | Giving our children a name | Page 64 |
| 17. | A study of local field names | Page 68 |
| 18. | Welsh surnames in Oswestry and district | Page 73 |
| 19. | Catering for Welsh speakers | Page 75 |
| 20. | A grand musical festival | Page 79 |
| 21. | Roberts the Gas | Page 81 |
| 22. | History reflected in stained glass | Page 86 |
| 23. | The builders of Plas Wilmot, Wilfred Owen's birthplace - their family background | Page 89 |
| 24. | Football crazy, football mad | Page 105 |
| 25 | George Bonner, artist and engraver | Page 107 |
| 26. | What's in a house name? | Page 114 |

## Introduction and acknowledgements

This is my eighth volume devoted to the history of Oswestry. The first, *Historic Oswestry*, was published in 1982, and the most recent, *An Oswestry miscellany*, in 2007. *Oswestry, a local history* was reprinted for the second time in 2013. My first published article was printed in the *Oswestry Advertizer* in January 1979, which seems a long time ago.

Oswestry is a very rewarding subject for historical research. It may be a relatively small town, certainly so in comparison with the major cities of England and Wales, or when set next to Chester or Shrewsbury for example. However, Oswestry has a history which belies its size, a history which reflects its strategic location on the English/Welsh border.

The twenty six chapters of the present volume have been taken, revised and supplemented by additional material as necessary, from the *Advertizer*, the *Salopian Recorder* (the journal of the Friends of Shropshire Archives), and from the Parish Magazine of St Oswald's and Christchurch, Rhydycroesau. I have also included a longer piece on the family history of Wilfred Owen, based upon a talk given to the Oswestry & Border History & Archaeology Group in 2017. The topics have been chosen so as to be varied in subject matter, and range across Oswestry's history from king Oswald to the twentieth century.

The intention is to present a portrait of Oswestry and district. The chapters include a number of studies of important Oswestrians including Hugh Yale, Edward Lloyd and Robert Roberts. Other chapters, whilst not focussing on a specific individual or particular local family, nevertheless seek to paint a picture of the town, to take our knowledge of Oswestry beyond the broad brush, towards a more detailed and in-depth examination of particular aspects of our collective history.

I am very grateful for the assistance provided by staff of Shropshire Archives, the National Library of Wales, Oswestry Town Council, and Oswestry Library, on numerous occasions, in relation to the various subjects included in this volume, and generally. I am also grateful to Oswestry Town Council for permission to reproduce three of the paintings in its collection, namely George Frederick Bonner's paintings of the Guildhall and Bailey Head, and the portrait of Robert Roberts; to the National Portrait Gallery for permission to reproduce the engraving of Archbishop James Ussher; and to the Cadbury Research Library, University of Birmingham, for permission to reproduce the illustration of the Yale Monument from the papers of William Mytton.

John Pryce-Jones
May 2020

## Illustrations

| | |
|---|---|
| St Oswald, as depicted on a church banner | Page 6 |
| The New Gate | Page 26 |
| The Yale Monument | Page 43 |
| Archbishop James Ussher | Page 51 |
| The Moses and Aaron triptych | Page 60 |
| Robert Roberts, gas proprietor | Page 83 |
| The Lawn, Church Street | Page 87 |
| Wilfred Owen's ancestry: | |
| • the descendants of Edward Salter and Mary Cross Simpson | Page 90 |
| • the Salter family | Page 92 |
| • the Cross family | Page 98 |
| Westgate House, Louth | Page 101 |
| Oswestry Guildhall, by G.F. Bonner | Page 112 |
| Glentworth, Morda Road | Page 115 |
| Houses in Morda Road | Page 116 |
| Street scene in Queen's Road | Page 118 |

A depiction of king Oswald, holding a cross and a sceptre, from one of the banners at St Oswald's parish church. Photograph © John Pryce-Jones.

## Chapter 1: Where exactly did king Oswald die?

Oswestry's links with St Oswald, king of Northumbria and Christian martyr, are well known. The mediaeval parish church is named after him. There is King Oswald's Well. The town itself is believed to derive its name from him. Historians are clear as to how Oswald died – killed in battle fighting king Penda of Mercia - and when – August 5th 642. Historians though are less certain as to where exactly he died. Although early chroniclers such as the 8th century monk the Venerable Bede in his *Ecclesiastical history of the English peoples* named the battlefield as "the place called in English *Maserfelth*", the location for this battle between the forces of Mercia and Northumbria is still a topic of disagreement and some controversy.

Some historians of Anglo-Saxon England note that *Maserfelth* is 'thought to be Oswestry'. Other writers are silent on the matter, or argue against Oswestry's claim. The late Dr Margaret Gelling, our foremost expert on place name origins, argued consistently that the name Oswestry was derived from an otherwise unknown local landowner called Oswald; she believed that the Normans chose Oswald as the patron saint for their new church because they were prompted by the pre-existence of the place name.

That said, there is significant evidence in our favour. The records of Shrewsbury Abbey indicate that Oswestry's parish church was already dedicated to St Oswald in the 1090s. Gerald of Wales, writing in the closing years of the 12th century, made the link between king Oswald and the names Oswestry and Croesoswallt. The *Life of Saint Oswald* written in the mid-twelfth century by the monk Reginald of Durham noted that *Maserfeld* lay close to Offa's Dyke and to Shrewsbury, that it belonged to Shrewsbury Abbey, that a church known as the white church had been erected near the site, and that the place had derived its name from St Oswald's tree. The earliest surviving reference to Saint Oswald's Well, in Oswestry, is found in a property deed of 1265.

However, there are other locations near and far which, like Oswestry, have a claim to be Bede's *Maserfelth*. Mediaeval Welsh histories – Nennius, the *Annales Cambriae*, and the 9th century poem *Canu Heledd*, gave the battle the name *Cocboy*, or *Maes Cogwy*, and have led in the past to arguments in favour of Coedway, a hamlet south of Melverley and just to the west of Alberbury, as the site of the battle.

Further afield, the parish of Winwick, in Ashton-in-Makerfield, south Lancashire, can cite as evidence the dedication of its mediaeval church, another St Oswald's, and the existence, a mile away, of another St Oswald's Well. It has also been argued that the name Makerfield might be derived from *Maserfelth*. These claims were debated by antiquarians in Victorian times – the merits of Winwick set out in the pages of *Local gleanings relating to Lancashire and Cheshire,* and in the Rev. Alban Butler's *Lives of the saints* (1866); the case for Oswestry put forward in *Bye-Gones* and in the *Transactions of the Shropshire Archaeological Society*. More recently, the volume *Oswald: Northumbrian king to European saint* (1995) examined the evidence, and the various arguments, very thoroughly, its authors concluding as far as they were able in Oswestry's favour[1].

That said, in the internet age, the issue remains very much a live one – just type 'Maserfelth' into Google to see. It is a live issue, though one that is unlikely ever to be wholly resolved, one way or another, unless a battlefield were to be found.

It is interesting, then, to consider the Staffordshire Hoard which was unearthed in a field between Brownhills and Lichfield, just off Watling Street (the present A5) in September 2009, and which caught the public's imagination, with lengthy queues inside and outside museums and galleries in Birmingham, Stoke and elsewhere when the treasure was first placed on display.

The hoard comprises more than 3,500 items, some of which are very small, made of gold, silver, and cloisonné garnets, and includes many fragments of sword hilts, with nearly a hundred pommel caps and a similar number of sword collars, along with decorative cheek pieces from helmets, and other martial objects[2]. The precise items each appear to have been deliberately bent, twisted or broken, before being buried together as a hoard – whether as part of a ritual, perhaps in thanks for victory in battle, or for safe keeping, with the intention of subsequent retrieval.

---

1  The location has also been discussed in detail by Max Adams, *The lion in the north: the life and times of Oswald of Northumbria* (2013)
2  These details have been revised in line with conservation work undertaken since the discovery of the hoard. The number of separate items has more than doubled from the figure given in the original article in February 2010

Despite all the interest, the discussion and the research, there remain many unanswered questions. Why was the treasure buried, and by whom? When exactly was it buried? When were the pieces made, and by whom? Initial consideration has tended towards the view that the hoard can be dated tentatively to the 7th or 8th centuries, and that it might represent 'booty' collected from the battlefield by victorious Mercian forces, stripped from the arms of the defeated forces of rival kingdoms, such as East Anglia and Northumbria. Experts have noted that Mercia was militarily aggressive and expansionist during the 7th century under its kings Penda, Wulfhere and Aethelred.

Oswestrians well know the story of king Oswald, and of the manner of his defeat by the pagan king Penda of Mercia. It seems very possible, perhaps even probable that the Staffordshire Hoard includes gold and silver collected from the battlefield at *Maserfelth* by Penda and his men, stripped from king Oswald and his Northumbrian army on August 5th 642, and interesting to note that, whilst the Staffordshire finds are almost exclusively martial, the hoard includes parts of two, or possibly three Christian crosses and a strip of gold which is inscribed with Latin text from the Old Testament Book of Numbers, chapter 10, verse 35. The Venerable Bede described how, in 634, king Oswald set up a cross before the battle of Heavenfield, north of Hexham; he was victorious on that occasion, so it is likely that he may well have done the same at *Maserfelth*, eight years later. This being so, it has been suggested that the strip of gold, with its Latin text, might have decorated the shaft of a cross, such as might have been carried at the head of an army as they marched forward into battle. The text would certainly have been appropriate for a warrior king such as king Oswald: "Rise up, O Lord, and may thy enemies be dispersed and those who hate thee be driven from thy face".

Oswestry can hope that, in time, the Staffordshire Hoard might provide firm evidence to help prove Oswestry's claim to be the site of the battle of *Maserfelth*; and that the Hoard really does represent booty – weapons, armour, Christian crosses – which formerly belonged to king Oswald and his forces, taken by Penda and his army from the battlefield on the Welsh border along Watling Street into the heart of Mercia.

*Based on articles printed in St Oswald's Parish Magazine for March 2010 and August 2011.*

## Chapter 2: Why Roft Street follows a crooked path – searching for St John's Hospital

It is surprising how aspects of a town's history, or major parts of the fabric of a town, can disappear entirely from view, with no trace surviving on the ground, and with no evidence found below ground either. In Oswestry's case, one such example is St John's hospital, which was an important feature of the life of the town for a span of three hundred years before it was closed down in the 1540s, with its assets sold off by the Crown.

St John's was founded in the first quarter of the 13$^{th}$ century by Bishop Reyner of St Asaph. Its origins are documented in the records of Haughmond Abbey[3] and make clear that the foundation was dedicated to both St John the Baptist and St John the Evangelist. Between 1200 and 1210, the bishop acquired lands in Oswestry from Shrewsbury Abbey upon which to build a hospital. He also bought other lands in and around the town to provide his foundation with a long-term income stream from the rent payments made by the tenants of these lands. The local clergy contributed a further nineteen acres; other churches including Llansilin also made donations; and Bishop Reyner continued to buy properties for the hospital, including several shops in Shrewsbury, until his death in 1224. In addition, William FitzAlan granted the hospital pasture rights in Cynynion, and the townspeople of Oswestry promised the hospital a handful of corn, flour or salt from every horse-load sold at the market, a gallon of ale from each brewing and a loaf from each baking.

St John's was not a hospital in the modern sense. Bishop Reyner set it up to provide a home for the poor and needy, and, in 1217, entrusted his foundation to the Knights Hospitallers of Halston, requiring them to maintain seven poor people there. However, soon after, there was a dispute between Halston and Haughmond over the running of St John's, resolved only by the intervention of Archbishop of Canterbury, Stephen Langton, who ruled that Haughmond should run the hospital, but pay Halston twenty shillings a year as a fee. Although this compromise lasted until the Reformation, surviving records show that Haughmond took a very limited view of its duties: by 1338, the hospital was leased to John de Rodenhurst, chaplain, who was required to provide a service on five days each week, maintain the buildings including a house, a chapel and a dovecote, and provide accommodation for visitors from Haughmond. His lease made no mention of the poor. Later, in 1468, Richard Ireland, gent., was awarded a 99 year lease of the "croft called Le Spitte Crofte in which the said chapel is situated". It is not clear whether that lease required the continued provision of services at the chapel.

---

3 U. Rees (ed.), *The cartulary of Haughmond abbey* (1985)

The hospital had remained largely unchanged for over 300 years, from its foundation until its closure in the 1540s. In the next forty years, in the reign of Elizabeth Tudor, documents show how the hospital changed hands several times[4]. Seized by the Crown, St John's was sold in 1560, along with other property of the Knights Hospitaller of Halston, to George Lee and George Bowyer of Shrewsbury. Six months later, they sold the "chapel of St John the Baptist and a close called Croft y Spytte" to Richard Jones of Oswestry, gent., whose son Thomas, in 1574, sold the property to Thomas Smalman of the Inner Temple, gent., the hospital described as "a house wherein the said Richard Jones lived at the time of his death in Oswestrye, [and] a meadow called Croft y Sputtye". In 1597, the lands changed hands again, when Smalman's son Stephen, another lawyer, sold the site to Hugh Maurice of Oswestry. The deed of 1597 describes the property as "a chapel called Saint Johns Chapple, two closes of land called Chapple Fieldes, otherwise Cae Capple Ieuan, lying adjacent to the said chapel, [and] land called Croft y Spyttu, otherwise The Croft of the Hospitall of St John". A later document, of 1780[5], records the sale of the site by Edward Maurice to John Croxon, and shows that the names *Chappell fields*, *Grofftydd Spythe* and *Roft y Sputtu* survived to that date. Other records, from the late 18th and early 19th centuries, confirm that fields known collectively as *roft-y-spytty* lay to the south of Roft Street on which were built Ferrers Road, Stewart Road and Park Street.

The principal reminders of the hospital today are the names St John's Court and Roft Street, the latter deriving from *roft-y-spytty*, or the hospital's croft. The hospital may have been dedicated to St John, but it was known from a very early stage simply as 'the spytty', from the Welsh *ysbyty*. One of the original Latin deeds, recording Bishop Reyner's purchase of land in Wilcott, indicates that the new hospital was already known as "le Sputti"; likewise, an agreement of 1265, also in Latin, describing a land swap between the abbeys of Shrewsbury and Haughmond, speaks of "la sputte". Even in the 13th century, Oswestry was culturally a Welsh town.

---

4   *Calendar of Patent Rolls, 1558-60* (1939), p273-274; National Library of Wales, Peniarth NB8 (1560), NB16 (1571), NB21 (1574), NB86 (1597)
5   Shropshire Archives, 4858/11,12

The precise location of St John's is not known. We have already seen that the lease awarded by Haughmond Abbey in 1338 referred to a house, chapel, and dovecote; the document also mentioned three crofts of land, and other unspecified buildings inside the hospital close. The antiquarian John Leland, who visited Oswestry in the late 1530s, described how "the chapel of St John the Baptist", lay "clene without the suburbes" and was situated "betwixt Stratllan [Church Street] and Porth De [the Black Gate]". Therefore, we know that it lay beyond the town walls, away from the ribbon development of Church Street and what later became Salop Road, and between Church Street and the Black Gate. There are hints in mediaeval deeds: one from 1332 describes a burgage plot in *Middelstrete* (which extended from the New Gate to the Cross) running back from the street as far as *Sputtys lane*[6]. Other deeds, of 1348, 1357 and 1381, describe tenements in *Chirton* (Church Street, from the 'Sun Corner' to the New Gate) which ran back from the street down to the meadow, or gardens of the "Sputty"[7].

Both historians and archaeologists tend to look with great interest at roads and property boundaries which stand out on a map or plan, either by forming a long straight line which cuts through the landscape (for example, the one marking the line of Wat's Dyke through from Llwyn Road to Oak Drive), or where a bendy line can be found amongst a mass of straight lines. Look at a map of Oswestry, or an aerial photograph, and the irregular course followed by Roft Street makes it stand out from its surroundings. It is likely that the sharp bend where Roft Street diverts away from its otherwise straight path around today's Regent Court, the former Croxon's Square, is telling us (or at least hinting at) something about the whereabouts of St John's hospital and its lands. Might the hospital's foundations survive buried beneath Regent Court, or under St John's Court nearby? If not there, might the foundations survive under the Memorial Hall, the premises of Marks & Spencer, or the Masonic Hall in Smithfield Road, all of which lie within the boundaries of the substantial grounds of the Croxons' home, The Lawn?

*Based on articles printed in St Oswald's Parish Magazine for May and June 2010*

---

6   SA, 6000/9039
7   NLW, Aston Hall 942, 2226; SA, 6000/9013

## Chapter 3: Local evidence of the Black Death

We all know of the Black Death, how it came to the British Isles having already spread east to west across Europe, and how between 1348 and 1350 it killed between a third and a half of the population. It was the cause of some villages being abandoned, and for a time caused serious upheaval in local and national affairs, as labour costs rose, and lords struggled to maintain their manorial rights as their tenants abandoned the land for opportunities elsewhere. The so-called Peasants' Revolt, in 1381, had some of its roots in the Black Death.

The disease moved fast, passing through the countryside, spread by human contact. It first arrived in England, on the Dorset coast, in June 1348, reaching Bristol by August and London by the Autumn. It spread remorselessly throughout the British Isles, all the way north to the Hebrides, Orkney and Shetland Isles. But when did the Black Death reach Oswestry, and what was its impact locally?

There are few local records from the 14th century in comparison with, say, the 16th century – no parish registers for instance, to list burials, day by day, as we have at St Oswald's for the outbreak of plague in 1559. The study of the Suffolk village of Walsham by Professor John Hatcher *The Black Death: the intimate story of a village in crisis, 1345-1350* is very firmly based on surviving records of manorial court sessions where the lord's steward would conduct business, including the transfer of land from generation to generation – and, of course, during these years, there were many more deaths, many more new tenants to be inducted. Another recent study of this period, Benedict Gummer's *The scourging angel: the Black Death in the British Isles* indicates that, for Shropshire, the pestilence reached Quatt, near Bridgnorth, by April 1349. Finally, the *Victoria County History* uses court rolls for Ruyton and Kinnerley to show that the Black Death was at its height in these parts during the summer and autumn of 1349.

Court records do not survive for Oswestry for this period. Nevertheless, we are fortunate that a number of 14th century property deeds survive, in libraries at Aberystwyth, Shrewsbury and Birmingham, including over ninety documents from the years 1329 to 1370 relating to the town of Oswestry, or to the adjacent rural townships of Sweeney, Weston Cotton and Llanforda[8]. Each of these documents is dated, right down to the day and the month, though following the manner of the time: the year based on the regnal year of the king (for instance 'the seventeenth year of the reign of king Edward III') and the precise date by reference to a saint's day ('the third day after the feast of St Michael the Archangel'). These deeds also tell us the names of many local people: those buying the land, those selling it, those who owned the neighbouring property – the house next door, the fields either side – as well as numerous other people who witnessed the transaction. Plotting the names included in each of these ninety documents against the date of each of the documents allows us to see when each of these individuals were alive, and to see how some names suddenly stop, whilst others continued on into later years, and this work can help us to confirm when the Black Death reached Oswestry.

A detailed analysis of these documents reveals that manorial officials and other leading townspeople such as John Lloyd son of Madog Fychan and his wife Emma, Roger le Roter, Richard de Haston, Philip Lestrange, Meurig ap Bleddyn, Iorwerth ap Bleddyn Lloyd, Griffith ap Einion Gethin and his wife Joan, all 'disappear' from the records at this time, indicating quite clearly that the plague reached Oswestry in the summer of 1349. The analysis also shows that many other people survived, their names appearing in documents both before and after the Black Death passed through the district – for instance William le Roter, Roger de Haston, Thomas Lestrange, Roger Morgan, Richard the son of Thomas le Salter, and Richard the son of William le Salter.

---

[8] City of Birmingham Library, Barnard MSS (various), NLW, Aston Hall MSS (various), SA, 6000/9017 to 6000/9070 (also 'Deeds relating to Oswestry', *Trans. Shrops. Arch. Soc.*, 53 (1949-50), p94-111), 'Welsh deeds', *Arch. Cambrensis*, New Ser., 9 (Jan. 1852), p36-45, Denbighshire Record Office, DD/WY/4616-4617, University of Birmingham, Cadbury Research Library, Mytton Papers, MYT/5/1001A

This period would have been a very busy, and a very traumatic time for the whole community, including the local clergy. *The Scourging Angel* shows how priests were particularly prone to infection by the plague because their duties brought them into direct contact with the sick and dying. To its credit, the church hierarchy worked hard to find replacement clergy, and to find additional support for priests working in plague-affected parishes. We do not know the name of our vicar in 1349, or how he fared when the plague struck. We know that Roger Harper was vicar of Oswestry in 1352 and the fact that his name appears in other documents of 1355, 1367 and 1371 shows that he served at St Oswald's for many years[9]. It may be that he was appointed vicar shortly after the plague had passed, to replace a predecessor who had been one of many local casualties of the Black Death.

Finally, it is interesting to note the movement of people in the aftermath of the outbreak. Across the country, the scale of casualties brought new opportunities to the survivors of the Black Death; they found themselves able to exploit their position during a labour shortage, and to take on tenancies for land suddenly made vacant due to the death of the previous tenants and their offspring. These ninety documents include the earliest reference to the Muckleston family in documents relating to Oswestry, a deed of 1357 referring to Roger de Muckleston[10]. The Mucklestons are likely to have had their origins in the parish of Mucklestone which straddles the Shropshire/Staffordshire border east of Market Drayton, and were to be active in the life of Oswestry for the next four hundred years and more. For example, William Muckleston was curate of St Oswald's in 1578; Richard Muckleston was vicar in 1612; and John Muckleston, a shoemaker, was mayor of Oswestry in 1692.

*Based on an article printed in St Oswald's Parish Magazine for February 2011, subsequently printed in a revised form in the Salopian Recorder, the newsletter of the Friends of Shropshire Archives, for Summer 2019*

---

9   'Welsh deeds', *Archaeologia Cambrensis*, New Ser., 9 (Jan. 1852), p41; City of Birmingham Library, Barnard 144/2; SA, 6000/9047, 6000/9052
10  NLW, Aston Hall 2226

## Chapter 4: Links to the court of king Henry VIII

There is an enduring fascination with the Tudors, with king Henry VIII and with the middle years of his reign, when the king's affections moved with rapid succession and immense consequence from Katherine of Aragon to Anne Boleyn and then to Jane Seymour. The novels *Wolf Hall* (2009) and *Bring up the bodies* (2012) by Hilary Mantel, and *The other Boleyn girl* (2001) by Philippa Gregory, and TV series such 'The Tudors' (2007/10) have focussed on the dynamics of the royal court, the rivalries between individual courtiers and noble families, and their desire to gain royal favour, to avoid falling out of favour, and to ensure that their own interests rose, if need be by engineering the downfall of others.

Quite clearly, the great changes at this time – the creation of the Church of England, the changes in the form of religion, the end of the monasteries, the abolition of chantries and religious guilds - had an immediate impact on St Oswald's, as they did on churches throughout England and Wales. However, one incident from this time will have had a more direct, more immediate impact, on the vicar of Oswestry at that time, Peter Brereton.

Appointed by 1529, and vicar until 1538 or later, Peter Brereton came from a highly influential Cheshire family. His father, Sir Randal Brereton of Malpas, had been created knight banneret in 1513 after Henry VIII's French campaign of that year, and had held the position of chamberlain of the county palatine of Cheshire. Also, Ralph Brereton of Iscoyd, the uncle of Sir Randal, had served the FitzAlans as steward of Oswestry from 1516 to 1529[11], and may have been instrumental in Peter's nomination as vicar.

Sir Randal, who died in 1530, had nine sons. Peter, the fifth son, trained as a priest. The sixth son, William, was one of four of the sons who were placed at court: he was there by 1521 and a groom of the privy chamber by 1524. His position at court, coupled with his landed interests in Cheshire and north Wales, meant that he became very wealthy. In 1529 William Brereton married the king's cousin Elizabeth, the widow of Sir John Savage, and in 1530 he succeeded his father as chamberlain of Chester. He had served as steward of the lordship of Chirk and Chirkland[12]. His powerful position on the Welsh border, seen at court as a lawless region, and a cause of concern, brought him into conflict with Thomas Cromwell, the king's chief minister, often seen as a scheming, or Machiavellian character.

---

11   J. Pryce-Jones, 'Stewards of the lordship of Oswestry from the 13th century to the Acts of Union of 1536 and 1543', *Trans. Shrops. Arch. & Hist. Soc.*, 80 (2005), p88
12   *Oxford dictionary of national biography* (2004), 7, p470-471

TV and film have documented the demise of Anne Boleyn, how she was unable to provide the king with a healthy son, and how she was then, perhaps conveniently, found guilty of committing adultery with a number of courtiers including Mark Smeaton, Sir Francis Weston, Sir Henry Norris, her brother Lord Rochford, and William Brereton, and executed on Tower Green on May 19th 1536. Brereton, almost certainly innocent, was arrested on May 4th 1536, tried and condemned on May 12th, and beheaded on May 17th. It has been suggested that Cromwell may have slipped Brereton's name onto the list of the accused simply to get him out of the way, seeing him as an obstacle to his reforms of the Marcher lordships. Machiavellian indeed.

What his brother Peter, serving his parish in Oswestry, well away from these tumultuous events in London, made of such events is not documented. The times being what they were, wisdom would have encouraged him to keep his head down, and to keep his views to himself, even if such an approach may have been out of character for the vicar: the records of the Court of Star Chamber, held at the National Archives at Kew, include a series of six cases, some brought by Peter Brereton, others where he is cited as the accused, concerning the right to collect the tithes of St Oswald's, which since the beginning of the 12th century had belonged to Shrewsbury Abbey[13]. The vicar argued against this arrangement, pointing out that he had been appointed to St Oswald's by the bishop of St Asaph rather than, as was then usual, by the abbot of Shrewsbury, "by reason that the churche was voyde". Bearing in mind the fact that surviving Star Chamber records provide arguments and counter arguments rather than objective truth, case records show vicar Brereton, with a large band of men from the lordship of Chirk, disrupting the collection of tithes in Oswestry by Thomas ap Meredith. They also show the vicar complaining to Star Chamber about the collection of tithes by the aforesaid Thomas, and later by Randall Ireland, on behalf of the abbot of Shrewsbury. These records show that the dispute had already been played out before the Princess Mary's council in the Marches of Wales, before the Lord Chancellor Cardinal Wolsey, and separately before the archbishop of Canterbury at the Court of Arches. We do not know the outcome of these disputes – although the vicar's evidence to the court suggests that he was arguing against previous court decisions in the abbot's favour.

---

[13] National Archives, STAC 2/6, STAC 2/34/2, STAC 2/18/42, STAC 2/24/223, STAC 2/20/80, STAC 2/20/76, also STAC 2/25/8

Other records show that Oswestry was not the vicar's sole interest.  As early as 1526 he had been appointed a chantry priest at the chapel of the Blessed Virgin Mary in St John's Church, Chester; later, in 1539, he complained to the king that revenue had been wrongfully withheld from the canons' chantry and that one of the chantry priests had been expelled unjustly.  In 1540, action was taken against the vicar for absenteeism under the statutes of 1529.  Again, the outcome is not known, but, when Peter Brereton died in March 1553, his will (which survives in the archives at Chester) included bequests to St Chad's, Malpas, where his parents were buried, to St John's in Chester, where he was to be buried, to St Oswald's, and to St Peter's, Heswall: it seems likely that he held office at these last three churches at the same time, remaining our vicar until his death, with his duties in Oswestry carried out by Owen ap David, a long-serving curate when Brereton was absent elsewhere.

Finally, we should note that Peter Brereton was very probably the founder of a wayside chapel, known as St Edith's chapel, which stood at the junction of Gobowen Road with Whittington Road, close to the parish boundary[14].  There are few references to it in historical records.   John Leland, the traveller and historian, in his *Itinerary* of England and Wales in the 1530s, provides one of the first references to the chapel, in his description of Oswestry, locating it "clene without the suburbes" and "north est toward Chester".  A brief survey of Oswestry, from the late 1530s or early 1540s indicates that the chapel was "bylt by the vicar of Oswestry and releeved by the inhabitants of the said Towne".  There are few other references to the chapel in surviving documents. The will of John Trevor of Oswestry, from 1541, refers to a croft "lying by Saint Edithe's chappell" and a survey of Oswestry compiled in 1602 notes that "the heirs of John Trevor have in their occupacion a litle peece of ground called the Chapel Peece lying at the point of theire land betweene two highe wayes whereof the one leadeth towards Westchester [Chester] th'other to Whittington parke [Park Hall]", the surveyor adding that "there was sometime a Chappell stoode upon this peece now decayed"[15].

---

14  The precise location of the junction 'moved' a little when the railway line and bridge were constructed in the late 1840s
15  NLW, Peniarth DG22; W.J. Slack (ed.), *The lordship of Oswestry, 1393-1607: a series of extents and rentals* (1951), p53

Wayside chapels, as St Edith's seems to have been, served the needs of travellers and, sometimes, of pilgrims, and were popular throughout the mediaeval period.  Few such chapels now survive, though they are a relatively common sight on the continent.  We cannot be sure when St Edith's was built, or by whom, but its dedication may suggest that its founder was Peter Brereton, whose family home, Ipstones, was close to the Norman church at Shocklach dedicated to St Edith of Polesworth.  If vicar Brereton was indeed the chapel's founder then St Edith's had but a short existence, as it seems likely that it was dissolved in the late 1540s during the short reign of Edward VI.

*Based on articles printed in St Oswald's Parish Magazine for October 2008, April 2010 and December 2010*

## Chapter 5: Sickness and plague in Tudor and Stuart times

That Oswestry experienced a major outbreak of plague in 1559 and 1560 is well known, with documentary evidence of the impact on local people provided by the parish registers and with the Croeswylan Stone, at the junction of Croeswylan Lane with Morda Road near to the Marches School, providing a physical reminder of those times[16]. Firm evidence to link the stone with these events is perhaps a little sketchy. The Rev. Peter Roberts of Ruabon, author of Price's *History of Oswestry* (1815), noted that "at this place is the base of an old cross, said to have been erected when the plague was in the town" adding that "during that time the market is said to have been held at this cross, lest the country people by coming in the town should be infected, or because of their fears if they did so". Isaac Watkin, in 1920, mentioned how the hollow left for the cross shaft had been used 'for many years' by 'country people' as a basin for collecting rainwater, in which they might wash their money. Although Watkin does not say so, presumably the purpose of their washing the coins was to avoid contagion. If so, the two stories are to some extent contradictory – either the cross was the focus for the displaced market, or the cross shaft had been removed by that time, leaving the base to form a wash basin.

Plague is one of those topics which can grab the attention and encourage thoughts of the macabre. Our perception of plague tends to be governed by what we know of much greater outbreaks, such as that of 1664/65 in London, described by Samuel Pepys and later by Daniel Defoe. It is clear that the circumstances in London forced the authorities to resort to mass burials, and that open land was used to create 'plague pits' in order to cope with the number of victims. In recent years, there has been speculation – and for some people seemingly a firm belief – that there is a 'plague pit' in Oswestry and that it lies under the Broad Walk. There is no evidence of such pits, nothing in the written histories of Oswestry, or in the surviving original source material. Given the enthusiasm of William Cathrall (author of the 1855 *History of Oswestry*) and Isaac Watkin for recounting a good story, it seems clear that rumours of plague pits were not circulating in their day, and it is reasonable, therefore, to cast great doubt upon the matter.

---

16  See *Historic Oswestry* (1982), p15-17, and *An Oswestry miscellany* (2007), p16-18.

It is interesting, and intriguing to understand how these tales seem to have entered the consciousness of modern-day Oswestrians, and very quickly to have become a 'fact' of our local history. There have been suggestions in the local press that a commemorative plaque should be placed in the Broad Walk marking the existence of plague burials hereabouts and, of course, were a plaque ever to be approved and to be fixed to the wall with due civic ceremony, the process would be complete – the historians' cause would be lost. That said, the death of around five hundred parishioners in 1559 and 1560 very clearly represents a noteworthy episode in our local history, and one which may well merit a memorial of some kind, but not one linked to a supposed location of a plague pit.

What *is* known is that the name Croeswylan predates the outbreak of plague. The name *Kroys welym* is mentioned in a deed of 1521; and a deed of 1484 refers to an unnamed cross standing in the highway from Oswestry towards Llanforda[17], which may well refer to Croeswylan; and it is possible that a reference in a deed of 1380 to *Crowylmot* also relates to this same location[18]. Although it is the case that in post-mediaeval times the names 'Croeswylan' and 'Croft Wilmot' came to signify respectively a cross base and a field at two separate locations along the Morda Road, it is possible that the two names had a common root – possibly *Croes Wilym* – Gwilym's or William's Cross - named after an unknown man who set it up. Setting that theory on one side, it has also been suggested that the second element of the name derives from the Welsh verb *wylo*, with Croeswylan meaning simply 'weeping cross'.

Whatever its role in time of plague, Croeswylan is likely to have been a wayside cross, erected at some stage in mediaeval times along what was one of the main routes into and out of Oswestry, and sited at the boundary between the liberties of Oswestry and the adjacent rural townships, where the traveller would enter or leave the town. It was one of several such sites in the area: in addition to the stone cross that stood in the centre of the town (at 'The Cross'), there was a small chapel dedicated to St Edith on the northern outskirts of the town (see chapter 4), and field name evidence suggests that another cross stood at Trefarclawdd beside the old road from Weston and Coedygo towards Llansilin. As is the case in many countries today, wayside crosses, and small roadside chapels or shrines, were a common sight in mediaeval England and Wales, until they were swept aside, or slighted, in the early years of the Reformation. In the case of Croeswylan, the shaft may have been removed, being broken up or re-used for building stone, leaving only the very heavy, and substantial cross base.

---

17  NLW, Aston Hall 2166 (1521); SA, 484/16 (1484). The present cross base stands on the boundary between the town of Oswestry and the township of Llanforda
18  City of Birmingham Library, Barnard 143/4

Plague was a comparatively frequent occurrence in Oswestry at this time. In addition to the outbreak in 1559/60, captured by the newly instituted parish registers, there was a second episode noted in the registers, where a contemporary margin note added by the vicar or curate indicated that "This yere the 18$^{th}$ daie of March 1585 the Plague began in this towne and contynued untill the 20$^{th}$ of July, whereof died three score and foure persons and no more"; there were ninety one burials in total during this period. While this outbreak was deemed worthy of a margin note, and described loosely as 'plague', analysis of the registers for the next thirty years reveals that this number of deaths was by no means a unique event in Oswestry's history. Insanitary living conditions, and an increasingly crowded town centre providing a home of a rapidly expanding population, brought about by thriving wool and leather trades, squeezing into the town's cramped mediaeval footprint, meant that diseases passed on by contact with others were able to flourish. Without the medicines that we take for granted, there was a wide range of diseases and illnesses which could lead to increased death rates, particularly among the very young and the elderly.

For example, there was a sudden increase in the number of burials towards the end of 1596, with seven deaths in September rising to twelve in October and a massive fifty one and forty one in November and December respectively. Although the monthly totals in the New Year had fallen back from these levels, the number of burials remained high throughout 1597, resulting in a total of 208 for the year compared with a 'normal' annual figure for the time of between 50 and 80. There was a second 'spike' in the annual totals in 1603, to 147 burials, with fifty seven of those burials occurring in April and May alone, and further 'spikes' in burial figures in 1613 (139 burials) and 1614 (126 burials). Whether these increased numbers each signify outbreaks of 'plague' is unclear, and perhaps unlikely. Some of the deaths would have occurred in any event. However, figures for neighbouring parishes including Whittington, St Martin's and Selattyn show broadly the same trends: in Whittington's case the three years with most burials were 1597 (56), 1603 (39) and 1614 (43), and it is apparent that something unusual had caused these increases – whether plague, influenza, typhus or, in the case of the 1596/97 increase, possible malnutrition brought about by famine due to grain shortages.

It is interesting to note that comparative figures for the Shrewsbury parishes of St Mary and St Chad present a different picture. In the case of St Mary's, there were increased numbers of deaths in 1597 and 1598, though to nowhere near the same degree as in Oswestry, and evidence of a significant outbreak of plague (described as such in their registers) in 1604, with 94 burials between June and September that year. In Oswestry, burials which had been at a high level throughout 1603 and into the spring of 1604, had returned to their normal levels by this time, suggesting that outbreaks could be very localised in their nature at this time.

Might any of these outbreaks have required the church to introduce the drastic measure of mass burials and plague pits, in the manner of outbreaks in London? There is no evidence to suggest that this was the case, and nothing in the surviving churchwardens' accounts for 1585, 1596/97, 1603 or 1613/14 that would suggest that the church failed to maintain 'business as usual' for burials during these periods. Whether this was possible in 1559/60 is less clear: certainly, it would have been a severe challenge for local church officials to cope with 256 deaths, to accommodate so many burials, in just two months, September and October 1559. Would the churchyard have been large enough, with sufficient space available for the number of burials? Probably it would; with sufficient manpower, it would not have been impossible; burials may have been simpler, taking up less space; and it was accepted practice that burial plots would be reused over the years.

If, however, there had been a need for emergency measures in 1559 or 1560, or at some other time, would the area later used for the Broad Walk have been chosen? It was part of the churchyard, so yes, it is possible, but it is just as possible that there were plague burials scattered throughout the churchyard. We need to bear in mind the fact that, until it was burnt down in 1644 during the Civil War, the vicarage stood on the site now occupied by Bellan House and its grounds, next to what is now the Broad Walk. Would the vicar have wanted a plague pit located so close to his home?

Also, it is thought possible that the brook that runs from Brynhafod Lane down Welsh Walls and then turns sharp left to run beside the Tennis Club into the Cae Glas park, used to follow a much more direct route from Welsh Walls, with its course following the line of the Broad Walk, across Church Street (or under it) to take the line of the private road through the Wynnstay Hotel grounds towards Roft Street, and beyond. If true, this might explain the curved line of the Wynnstay's boundary wall, and would have meant that the boundary between the churchyard and vicarage in the 16$^{th}$ century was formed by a brook. If this was the case, would plague burials have been contemplated so close to a stream?

*Based on articles printed in St Oswald's Parish Magazine for October 2007, January 2014 and April 2016*

## Chapter 6: Eye witness tales of an attempted *coup*

Viewed from a distance of four hundred years or more, the transition of our local government arrangements from seignorial administration on behalf of the lord of the manor to locally managed civic administration can appear one of a steady progress, a series of steps to reach a known outcome: moving forward from the Book of Constitutions of 1582, to the borough charter of 1617, the Charles II charter of 1673, the upheaval in local government brought about by the Municipal Corporations Act of 1835 and so on to the present day.

However, the detailed evidence provided by four cases taken to Star Chamber between the late 1550s and 1585[19] shows that the path was sometimes a bumpy one and the outcome far from certain. At that time civic government in Oswestry was headed by two bailiffs, elected annually on the Friday after Michaelmas "in the common hall or elecc'on howse" within the New Gate. However, there was disagreement among the burgesses, between those who favoured election by all the burgesses, and those who advocated election by the leading burgesses only. The controversy first surfaced at Star Chamber, when the bailiffs for 1560, Thomas Evans and John Stanney, "very faccious and busye headed p'sons", were accused by Henry, the last FitzAlan earl of Arundel, of changing the election procedures to suit their own needs. Evans and Stanney were "comytted to the flete [prison], disenfranchesed of ther fredome, their names [to] be blotted or raced out of the Registers booke of the towne and they from thensforth [were to] paye toles tallage and other duties".

In 1580, on the death of Henry FitzAlan, a group of leading townsmen, mainly members of the mercers' company, tried again. They felt that elections open to all burgesses led to "contenc'ons and suytes in lawe between the Burgesses to the great decaie of the Towne". The same Thomas Evans, and Richard Williams, who were the bailiffs for 1581, negotiated with officials of Philip Howard, the new earl, for a set of rules for the government of the town, subsequently known as the Book of Constitutions. These rules gave "full power and aucthorytie to xxv of the most substancallest & discreatest Burgesses" concentrating power in the hands of a Common Council of twenty five men – largely men from the leading merchant families of the town – thereby excluding less influential burgesses. The new rules were presented to the townspeople as a *fait accompli* on June 8th 1582.

---

19  National Archives, STAC5/A48/18, STAC5/S35/19, STAC5/W44/28, STAC5/M59/30

The new arrangements were not universally popular. As soon as the book was published, the vicar, the Rev. John Price, and others including Griffith Kyffin, spoke out against the changes claiming that these reforms disadvantaged the common burgesses and townspeople, to the benefit of the leading merchant families. The vicar was a local man whose father John ap Thomas ap Rhys and grandfather Thomas ap Rhys had both served as bailiff; his elder brother Robert Pryce had been bailiff in 1577, and was one of the 'twenty five' that made up the Common Council in 1582. The vicar died in March 1583 and his will shows clearly his connections to some of Oswestry's leading families, such as the Smallmans, the Drihursts, and the Lloyds of Drenewydd; he may also have been related to the Stanneys.

The vicar was not a stranger to controversy: in the late 1550s, the vicar and John Lloyd, probably of Llanforda, were accused by the earl of Arundel of undermining regulations relating to bread and baking in the town. Taking his case to Star Chamber, the earl had described them as "greate workers of disturbens, contentions, sedycion and troble within the town", accusing them of "intending to subverte and overthrowe the said good orders" by stirring up "sedycion, mutanye and stryffe". He claimed that they had gathered together, with around twenty men "beinge of the worste & moste disorderly people", and had proceeded to alter the price of goods – bread, corn, grain, beer and ale – as well as to encourage non-payment of rents and dues payable to the earl and, very interestingly, to "pull down hedges, ditches and enclosures". The vicar had also written and distributed "dyvers wrytynges and pamphletts conteyninge his saide sedycyous and unlawfull practices".

Returning to the controversy caused by the new Book of Constitutions, the bailiffs for 1584, Roger Stanney and Richard Cowper, along with other councillors such as Hugh Yale, told Star Chamber that "one John Price clerke, deceased, late vicar ... and Griffeth Kyffyn ... who hadd married the nease of the said John Price, with Richard Kynaston and William Goughe" had encouraged opposition to the new set of rules. The bailiffs claimed that the vicar "did geve oute speeches against the said Booke of Constitucions and raysed a most untrewe rumor", as noted above, "that ... the comon burgesses, people and inhabytantes of the Towne were and should be brought into such Thraldom that they shold neyther buy nor sell lynnen nor woollen clothe as before they did". They said that the vicar had also claimed that "the said Booke was procured for the pryvate welthe of the said fyve and twentie personnes of the comon councell".

Stanney and Cowper claimed that the vicar's intervention had provoked the townspeople, and the rank and file burgesses, so that one of their number, John Morys, "being a busye [factious] fellow and of the [faction] of the said Price, Kiffen, Goughe and Kinaston", had in November 1584 made a complaint about the new constitution to Star Chamber "against the said xxv p'sonnes for the overthrowe of the Booke of orders & quyet governem't".  Star Chamber ordered both sides to wait upon the earl, to make their case to him.  John Morys attended the earl's London house, on the Strand, but was told that his rivals Richard Williams and Hugh Yale had already received the earl's decision on the matter.  Morys asked Williams and Yale for a copy of the decision, but "they denied and refused to shew hime" telling him that the earl had decreed that "all & anye the Burgesses shold observe and obey the orders contained in the booke of Constituc'ons, all and anye clause article & sentence therein contained" until the lord's officials next visited Oswestry.

An eighteenth century engraving of the New Gate, looking through the gateway towards Church Street and the parish church.  The large window above would have brought light to the burgesses' hall.

This was the situation in 1585 as the designated election day, October 1st approached.

For the common councillors, the 1585 election was a case of business as usual: "Roger Stanney and Ric' Cowper then bailiffs with others of the common councell repayred in quiet & cyvell order to the comon hall" and elected Richard Williams and Thomas Kynaston as bailiffs. However, for the 'lesser' burgesses, rebuffed by Star Chamber, out-manoeuvred by the twenty five, rejected by the earl and his officials, it was a case of deciding what to do next. They looked back to June 1582, when they had pressed for changes to the new constitution to require the common council to be elected afresh by all the burgesses every three years. Three years had now expired, and therefore, "since there was noe order sett downe so fare as they could knowe or understand by the Earle", they concluded that "yt was the meetest course to followe the anncient man' and forme of ellection w'ch had so longe contynewed".

Answering questions posed by Star Chamber, Morys and his allies claimed that "upon the frydaie next after michallmas daye [they] did in quiet and seemly order accordinge to their ancient usage repayre unto the comon hall of the towne and did p'ceede to the elecc'on of the bayliffes and officers by the voice of all or the greatest p'te of the burgesses by w'ch elecc'on the said Rondell Lloyd and Griffith Kyffyn were orderly chosen baliffes". As was so often the case at Star Chamber, the complaint and the response to it were poles apart.

It seems that "Randle lloyde and Griffeth Kyffen beinge two of the xxv, w'thout any regarde of their Corporall othes" had absented themselves from the common hall at the time of the election of Williams and Kynaston so as to "conspire and confederate" with forty eight named burgesses, including John Morys, "to overthrowe the orders or constituc'ons". Joining "divers other willfull ryotous and disordered p'sonnes to the number of fower score p'sonnes beinge in warlike manner armed with daggers & other weapons and [with] others of their adherency [hidden] in shoppes howses and cellars in severall places w'thin the Towne" they had invaded the election house. There, they "did exclaime against the comyne councell and against the Bayliffes w'ch [had just been] elected protestinge with greate othes that [the councillors] shold ioyne with them and proceede to a newe elecc'on", threatening that "they wold make the common council eyther yeld their assente or ells make them starve [keeping them] w'thout meat drinke fire or candle untill they wold assent".

They "did mock or deryde the Bayliffes and those that were of the Comon Counsell by callinge for nightcappes" and by suggesting that "they might stop mustard pottes with their newe book of constituc'ons". They locked the councillors in, fixing padlocks to the doors of the election hall, and set "greate iron chestes stones tymber and other suche thinges" against the door, so that none of the common council could leave "by the space of two daies and onne nighte". Knowing that many of the twenty five were "very aged quiet p'sonnes and some of them very sickly & impotent p'sons", they "did in the night seison rune upp & down the hall drawing after them a greate iron plough chayne with suche noyce and outcries that none cold take any rest" and, when friends of the councillors attempted to get food through to them, they threatened "to cast them over the walles and thereby to breake their necks to the greate terror uprore & disquietinge of the Towne". Meanwhile, "the disordered p'sonnes themselves hadd their victuales".

As a result, Griffith Kyffin and Randle Lloyd, members of the common council but also members of long-established local families, were elected bailiffs. This is confirmed by the Bailiffs' Book, part of Oswestry Town Council's archives[20], which records that on October 15th the new bailiffs and their supporters had to break open the town chest, because the previous bailiffs had refused to hand over the borough records. However, they found no charters there, only "ii boxes, with some lettres in them, the towne seale and ii pap' bookes". Their election is further confirmed by the complaint made by twelve councillors to Star Chamber which has provided much of the eye-witness detail to this event.

Although the Star Chamber proceedings are silent on the outcome of the case, the Bailiffs' Book records that on May 8th 1586 the bailiffs of 1584 Roger Stanney and Richard Cowper finally handed over the borough records to their successors Thomas Kynaston and Richard Williams: clearly, they had withheld them from Griffith Kyffin and Randle Lloyd for the past seven months. Kyffin and Lloyd had served as bailiffs for only part of the year, though the fact that Mr Kyffin was elected bailiff again in 1587, and Mr Lloyd in 1588, suggests that Star Chamber may have achieved a compromise between the two parties.

---

20  Oswestry Town Council, A12

It is interesting to consider why the vicar took the stance that he did in this dispute, this mini *coup*. Was his alliance with Richard Kynaston, William Gough and Griffith Kyffin, like his earlier association with John Lloyd of Llanforda, an indication that he was part of Oswestry's old order, whose authority came from their landed interests and their families' long-established status, and that they were concerned at the increasing influence of a new merchant class? Or was his concern, and those of his allies Kynaston, Gough and Kyffin, more altruistic, and focussed on the interests of the seemingly disenfranchised lesser burgesses, who belonged to the less influential trades?

*Originally printed in the Salopian Recorder, the newsletter of the Friends of Shropshire Archives, for Autumn 2008; other details taken from articles printed in St Oswald's Parish Magazine for April and May 2008*

## Chapter 7: An Elizabethan service contract

We tend to think of the service contract as a comparatively recent phenomenon. We pay a sum each month, or each year, to guarantee a prompt response if things go wrong, say, with our gas boiler or computer. Like so many other aspects of contemporary life, the service contract is in fact a concept with a long history and evidence from the records of Oswestry parish church[21] shows that the practice was one that our forefathers four hundred years ago understood and utilised.

In November 1591, the four churchwardens at St Oswald's for that year - William Lloyd, Thomas Iveson, John Jenyns and John David ap Nicholas - reached written agreement with John Priest of Bewdley in Worcestershire to mend the church clock. He agreed for a fee of twenty six shillings and eightpence "to come and repair the clock for a whole yeare space upon his owne charges if any fault be by his workmanship". The same month one of the two bailiffs of the town, Robert Edwards, the deputy bailiff Griffith Kyffin, and the same four churchwardens signed a similar agreement with John Lloyd of Denbigh, a glazier, "to keepe and sufficiently repayre the glasse windows of the parish church of oswestre continually from yeare to yeare as longe as he can worke and so to keep it in reparation twise a yeare that is at the Nativitie of our lord & the feast of pentecost", for the sum of thirteen shillings and fourpence.

The agreement with Mr Priest appears only to have lasted a couple of years as, in 1594, St Oswald's commissioned Adam Bradshaw of Shrewsbury, described as a blacksmith, to make a brand-new clock. Four years later, a further agreement was reached with Mr Bradshaw that, upon eight days' notice, he would travel over from the county town to repair the clock. Other agreements are recorded in the churchwardens' accounts with the plumber John Pellitorie of Shrewsbury, who was contracted to maintain all the lead on the church roof, and two local men Edward ap Ieuan (or Edward Tyler) and his son Elis ap Edward, who were slaters. The father and son team agreed, for an initial payment of forty five shillings a year and subsequent annual fees of twenty six shillings and eightpence, "to keepe and repayre all the tyle worke hanginge over the whole body of the church of oswestre and to fynd lyme morter and mosse and stones and all other necessaries whatsoever savinge only the cariadge of stones to be provided by the church wardens upon the chardges of the parishioners".

---

21  W. Day (ed.), *The churchwardens' accounts for 1579-1613* (1970)

With the exception of the arrangement for the maintenance of the slate roof, the common factor in these contracts is that these were with men from elsewhere. The implication is that Oswestry, at that time, did not have those skills readily available within the town – and therefore it was important for the church to have identified someone that they could call upon at short notice if the need ever arose.

Turning back to the glazier John Lloyd, the churchwardens' accounts record only two other payments to him, one for thirty three shillings and tenpence "for mendinge of the church glass windowes", before the work was transferred to another man. The accounts for 1592 record a payment of seventeen shillings "paid to hardinge the glasier of Salope for mendinge the glasse windowes", and in 1594 thirty three shillings and fourpence paid "to hardinge the glasier for mendinge the glaste windowes" and twelve shillings and sixpence "for glasinge the nue window". Finally, in 1597 there is a payment of eighteen pence "to the glacier of shrosbery for his travell hither" and a further twenty one shillings and twopence for glazing work.

It is easy to imagine both the churchwardens' frustration at having to pay extra charges for travel, there being no-one more local to do the work, and also the opportunity presented to local craftsmen, and men from elsewhere to set up business in Oswestry to meet the emerging needs of the church, and of the town generally. In this context it is interesting to see that, after Mr Harding, the parish church was able to use a local glazier, Walter Benet. Mr Benet was very probably not a native of Oswestry, but references in the parish registers show that he was living in the town: the registers for July 5th 1601 recording the baptism of "Abraham the sonne of Walter Benet glasier", and on June 4th 1602 the infant Abraham's burial. He is mentioned in the churchwardens' accounts for 1604, paid sixteen shillings and eightpence "for mending of the window in church 5th of march" and in 1605 five shillings and tenpence "to the glasier water Benet three skore & Tenne pownds of lead beinge the church lead". Shortly afterwards, on June 1st 1605, the churchwardens agreed a contract with Mr Benet, paying him twenty six shillings and eightpence a year "during his abode in Oswestree to mayntayne in good reparacion not only the whole glass windows about the church but also the whole leads hanginge over the whole body of the church and steeple". He was to find "all necessaries therunto belonginge, as glass, lead and soder" at his own cost, except where new leads needed to be cast. This contract remained in force for the next five years, as the accounts for subsequent years show a series of part payments, of ten shillings, twenty shillings, or six shillings and eightpence. The last time that Mr Benet was mentioned in the accounts was in August 1610 when the churchwarden Edward Kynaston paid twenty pence "to walter benet his man for saudringe the Leads". In 1611, the records note a payment of sixteen shillings "to John Lloyd glasier for glasing and amending the church wyndowes" – though whether this refers to the John Lloyd employed in 1591, twenty years earlier, or to a different man is not clear.

It is worth noting too that surviving records of Oswestry's company of corvisers[22], or shoemakers' guild, indicate that Walter Benet belonged to that company, and was a master within it: those records show that in 1610 he took on his son Richard as an apprentice. Oswestry did not have a separate company for plumbers and glaziers (it would have been very small), and it is possible that Mr Benet was allowed to join the corvisers, not as a shoemaker but as a fellow craftsman. It is very unlikely that there were two Walter Benets in Oswestry at this time.

Finally, records of the Chester City Quarter Sessions include papers from August 6th 1611 relating to an "examination concerning an apprentice of Walter Bennett glazier who ran away from his master because of ill treatment". Again, does this suggest that there were two Walter Benets, both glaziers, living only 25 miles or so apart, or had Oswestry's Walter Benet moved on again, to Chester, where no doubt there were more opportunities for an ambitious glazier?

*Based on articles printed in St Oswald's Parish Magazine for November and December 2011*

---

22  NLW, 9237E. For details of the corvisers, J. Pryce-Jones, 'Social and economic factors at work in Tudor and Stuart Oswestry: the records of the corvisers' company of Oswestry', *Trans. Shrops. Arch. & Hist. Soc.*, 80 (2005), 103-112

# Chapter 8: Looking back on Oswestry in the year 1611

*The year 1611 saw the publication of the landmark translation of the Bible now generally known as the King James Bible.*

What do we know of Oswestry, or of St Oswald's church, four hundred years ago, in 1611? We know that Oswestry was, as it remains, a Welsh border market town, part of Shropshire yet also part of the Welsh Marches. At that time, Oswestry played a pivotal role in the Welsh wool trade, which was critical to the prosperity of the town and district – both for the merchants, and for the weavers, dyers and other tradesmen who relied upon the market, held in the town's streets each Monday. Alongside the wool trade, many Oswestrians worked in leather – as tanners, shoemakers or glovers. Agriculture dominated the countryside; also, there were several working mills, and in the Morda Valley some small-scale coal mining. The town was still dominated by its castle, the town walls protected by a deep outer ditch, and the four gateways allowing traffic into the walled town. Beyond the walls, St Oswald's dominated the skyline, as it does now – except that the church tower was surmounted by a spire, or more likely by a central turret. The parish served by St Oswald's was much larger then – extending south to Treflach and Crickheath, and west to Pentregaer and Cynynion.

It is very helpful that many contemporary records have survived. For the church, there are the parish registers, and the churchwardens' accounts. For the town, there are civic records, some court records, property deeds and some wills. We know that the vicar in 1611 was Nathaniel Tattersall whose brother Philip was the sexton or parish clerk. We know that the four churchwardens at the start of the year were William Cowper, Richard ap Hugh of Sweeney, Edward Kynaston of Maesbury and the glover Hugh ap Cadwaladr; at Pentecost, these four were replaced by Richard Parry, John Morgan, Thomas ap John Thomas, and a fourth, unknown man. We know that the two bailiffs, who sat at the head of the corporation, were William Cowper and Richard Jones, who were replaced at Michaelmas by William Heilyn and William Morris. Protecting the bailiffs as they carried out their role, in the council chamber, the court house and in the streets of Oswestry, were two sergeants at mace, or mace bearers; these were Richard Marcroft and Roger ap Thomas. The lord of the manor was Thomas Howard, earl of Suffolk whose local interests and responsibilities were carried out by a steward; from November 1610, this was Sir John Townshend, who had replaced the local man Edward Lloyd of Llwynymaen.

These were challenging years for St Oswald's, and for Oswestry. The churchwardens' accounts show that Vicar Tattersall's ten years at St Oswald's were littered with disputes, aired at St Asaph, and in the courts of the Welsh Marches and London. The records of the court of Star Chamber in particular paint a picture of on-going strife between the key players, including the vicar himself, the sexton, the wardens, the bailiffs, the steward, the sergeants and many others. These were very litigious times. In October 1610, in a dispute over the position of sexton, the church and church tower had been locked against the vicar, who had then broken in, using ladders and entering through a window in the tower. The vicar's brother Philip and the wife and daughter of Thomas Edwards, his rival as sexton, had come to blows (an episode described in more detail in *Oswestry: parish, church and people*). A libellous verse had also been written and published against Edward Lloyd who had in turn complained that the church bells had been rung for joy in November at his replacement as steward.

These disputes continued through into 1611. Lloyd claimed that he stayed away from the town throughout December and into January, to avoid provoking further unrest, until things came to a head on and around Sunday January 20$^{th}$ when the vicar read out a writ of excommunication, under the seal of the bishop, against Lloyd, his wife, his mother-in-law, his children Richard and Jane, and Jane Smallman, a servant, for recusancy "and not repayring to churche to heare devine service". The same day, Lloyd rode into town with two of his menservants, on urgent business: a warrant for the arrest of the vicar – which was handed to the bailiffs but not carried out. Lloyd also issued a warrant against the bailiffs themselves, in relation to their failure to deal with the theft of a kettle, worth half a crown, on St Andrew's eve last November. Later the same day, at about seven o'clock, when the bailiff Richard Jones was preparing for bed, he was summoned by the vicar's brother shouting "murder, murder" and claiming that Lloyd's servants were attacking the vicarage, breaking down the gate and door. The bailiffs attended, questioned the vicar, and then visited the nearby house of William Baylie, to question and arrest Lloyd's servants, who were subsequently held captive at the home of the widow Griffiths (mother of the sergeant, Roger ap Thomas).

These details – which are merely the edited 'highlights' of events at that time, but which provide a flavour of local life - explain the gap in the parish registers between February 19th and August 3rd 1611, and for most of January 1612 highlighted sternly in the register with the comment "Here wantest a Regester for fyve months by the negligence of Mr Nathaniell Tattersall Vicar". They also provide the context for Mr Tattersall's fall in May 1612 when he was deprived of the living "for grave crimes" and heinous misdemeanours, and "degraded from all other spiritual promotions" by the church courts, being replaced as vicar by Richard Muckleston.

The churchwardens' accounts for 1611 and 1612 do not include any payments for a new Bible and, as these records only survive to 1613, with some loose sheets to 1615, they do not reveal when exactly the church acquired a copy of what became known as the King James Bible. It seems that copies of the new Bible could be purchased for ten shillings in loose leaf form, or twelve shillings bound. However, the churchwardens' accounts do show that St Oswald's had spent thirty shillings on a new Bible, plus a shilling for carriage, in October 1607, so one might imagine a sense of mild frustration tempering the wardens' great expectation as they found that their expensive new Bible had been superseded so quickly by the new authorised edition.

*Based on an article printed in the booklet produced by St Oswald's to commemorate the 400th anniversary of the King James Bible*

## Chapter 9: Edward Lloyd of Llwynymaen, a very difficult man

Details set out in the previous chapter illustrate how Edward Lloyd of Llwynymaen was one of the leading players in a series of local disputes, during the reign of king James I, involving the vicar of Oswestry, the vicar's brother Philip Tattersall, then the parish clerk, and other prominent characters in civic life at the time, described in detail in *Oswestry: parish, church and people* (2005). Mr Lloyd was a difficult man, and evidence, from papers in the Town Council archives, from the records of the Court of Star Chamber[23], and from the short biographies of him in the online *Dictionary of Welsh biography* and the *Oxford dictionary of national biography*[24] makes clear that he was a challenge to get along with, and also hard to fathom.

The son of Richard Lloyd of Llwynymaen, he trained as a lawyer at the Inner Temple in London and, after the earl of Suffolk was granted the lordship of Oswestry in 1602, was appointed the earl's steward. His appointment was something of a 'poisoned chalice', as Lloyd took on the task of enforcing the earl's rights, collecting the earl's rents and securing the earl's assets in Oswestry, after a period when those rights had been managed more loosely. His duties would have made him unpopular, more so because, unusually for the role of steward, he was a local man, who lived locally.

Clearly being local had its advantages, as he would know the territory, and be much more difficult to fool or outwit, but it meant that the likely natural animosity of the lord's Oswestry tenants towards the lord's steward acquired a more personal, and practical side. Also, the fact that he belonged to a long-established local family, was conscious of his status as a gentleman, as steward and as a justice of the peace, and had a haughty, perhaps a superior manner, would not have helped. However, the additional factor that turned all these circumstances into a really toxic mix was religion, and the known Roman Catholic sympathies of Edward Lloyd and his family. Lloyd's father Richard was listed in official records from 1592 as a recusant (that is, someone who refused to attend services of the Church of England); earlier, in 1575, he had been implicated, along with the vicar John Price and Henry, earl of Arundel, in government investigations into the whereabouts of a Catholic agent Hugh Owen. In 1577, a survey of Oswestry shows that Richard Lloyd was then out of the country, living in Flanders. He died in March 1602, when Edward Lloyd would have inherited his land and property in Oswestry and Llwynymaen.

---

23   Including STAC 8/198/15, STAC 8/198/25, STAC 8/198/26, STAC 8/198/27, STAC 8/205/21, STAC 8/205/22, STAC 8/207/20 and STAC 8/207/35
24   https://biography.wales; *Oxford dictionary of national biography* (2004), 20, p184-185. The latter misidentifies the Edward Lloyd of the Parliamentary controversy as of Berth-lwyd, Montgomeryshire

As the steward, Lloyd was a powerful figure in the town. However, once he had been replaced as steward in November 1610, he became vulnerable. At this point, the vicar felt able to complain about Lloyd's actions in October 1610 when he had assembled in the churchyard, with twelve associates, and had entered the church to change the locks. The vicar alleged that at this moment his "curate was very busie in reading of devine service and performing the usuall Rites of Christian buriall to the dead corps of a parishioner there to be interred in the churche porche". Lloyd, he said, "did verie unreverentlie (not once uncovering his head) whiles the curat was reading the prayers and solempnties of burial rudelie stepp over the grave or pitt wherin the dead corps was to be buried". The vicar claimed that, with the locks changed, he had been unable to enter the church, had no access to his books, and was unable to read divine service or to visit the sick for a fortnight. As noted in chapter 8, in January 1611, the vicar received orders from the bishop of St Asaph to read out, openly in church on January 20$^{th}$, a writ of excommunication of Lloyd, his wife Joan, his mother-in-law Susan Neame, his children and a house servant "for popish recusancy" and not attending church services.

Later that year, Lloyd claimed that his enemies in Oswestry had "faulsly, maliciously and wickedly" informed the Lord President of the Marches of Wales, in Ludlow, that Lloyd "did keepe and maintaine a seminary priest in his house [at Llwynymaen] knowinge him to be a seminary priest".

Accusations of this serious nature risked Lloyd's life and, as he noted, the forfeiture of his estate "to his utter undoing and overthrow of him his wyffe and children". Privy Council ordered a commission to sit in Oswestry to hear evidence against him, and a neighbour of Lloyd's, John ap Edward ap Richard, from nearby Sychtyn, informed the commissioners that, nine years earlier, on the death of Elizabeth I, Lloyd had spoken ill of the queen, saying that it was a pity she had lived so long, and claiming that she had had several children. As with many cases taken to Star Chamber, it is far from clear how much of the evidence was based upon truth – but the fact that these claims were being made against Lloyd at this time says something about the atmosphere in Oswestry. Unsurprisingly Lloyd was summoned before the Privy Council in London to explain himself – though it seems no further action was taken at that time.

Given the rumours circulating about him, and his own undoubted awareness of the risks they posed to his life and his family's well-being, why did he choose to speak out against Sir Francis Eure, a judge on the north Wales circuit (and his neighbour at Brogyntyn) in 1619 so that he found himself placed in gaol, first in the Tower of London and then in the Fleet prison? And why, when already in prison, did he speak out against the king's daughter, the princess Elizabeth, after her husband's Protestant forces had been defeated by a Roman Catholic army in Bohemia? As a result, Lloyd found himself in May 1621 condemned by both the House of Commons and the House of Lords, with the two houses vying, in a parliamentary *cause célèbre*, as to which chamber was empowered to try him, and which could punish him the more severely. He was fined the enormous sum of £5,000, degraded from the rank of gentleman, branded and sentenced to life imprisonment (though in fact he was released in July 1621). His wife Joan petitioned the king for the release of his books and papers, which were returned in December 1621 except for some "popish beads and popish books".

It is thought that Edward Lloyd returned to Llwynymaen and lived there into his old age. Joan died in 1636, and was buried at St Oswald's. It is not certain when exactly Edward Lloyd died – though the years 1648 or 1649 have been suggested – and likewise it is not clear where he was buried, as there is a gap in St Oswald's parish registers from 1640 to 1653. His son Richard, a Royalist commander in the Civil War, was buried in the parish church in February 1664.

*Based on articles printed in St Oswald's Parish Magazine for March and April 2012*

# Chapter 10: Hugh Yale and the Yale Monument

There is a story in Isaac Watkin's *Oswestry*, taken from Thomas Owen's *Reminiscences*, about the Rev. George Cuthbert[25]. He was a curate at St Oswald's from 1853 to 1873, during the long period when the then vicar, the Rev. Thomas Salwey was absent due to poor health. The story is that Mr Cuthbert met Charles Sabine, a local solicitor, in the Broad Walk "one bitterly cold winter's day with a deep snow on the ground". Mr Sabine told the curate how he had just left "a scene of misery and desolation such as I have seldom witnessed ... two poor old people without a particle of food or fuel, both kneeling in the attitude of prayer before a bare table". He continued, "I assure you the stony gaze of that poor old couple will not soon be forgotten by me". The curate was shocked and asked for their names so that he could visit them. Mr Sabine, in a stage whisper, told him they were "Mr & Mrs Yale" and hurried away before the penny could drop.

The story shows how familiar we are with Mr & Mrs Yale, Hugh and Dorothy, whose impressive monument has stood in our parish church ever since the reign of king James I. We know, too, that our Hugh Yale was a relation, an ancestor of the founder of Yale University in the United States, Elihu Yale.

But how much more do we know about Hugh Yale? Local parish registers show that he died in 1606, recording his burial on January 9$^{th}$. The churchwardens' accounts record small payments made for the ringing of the church bells at his funeral, and for the making up of his grave, and list a payment of twenty shillings in 1606 "by the hands of mrs yale bequethed by her husband mr hughe yale towards the reparacion of the church". The accounts also show that in 1608 Mrs Yale was receiving communion at home: there is a payment of a penny for the wine.

The earliest reference to Hugh Yale in surviving records of Oswestry dates from the early 1570s. Three related documents held at Shropshire Archives, from February 1571, show that he was one of the signatories to a marriage agreement between prominent local families[26]. Corporation records held by the Town Council show that he was elected a burgess of Oswestry in 1578, and that, from that time on, he played a prominent role in civic affairs. He was bailiff (equivalent to Mayor) in 1578 and 1582, and was central to the controversial reform of the common council in the 1580s. Court records show that with another councillor, Richard Williams, he was entrusted with the task of attending on the earl of Arundel at his Thames-side palace on the Strand in November 1584. The same records show that he sought to keep the common

---

25  I. Watkin, *Oswestry* (1920), 38-39, T. Owen, *Personal reminiscences of Oswestry fifty years ago* (1904), 39-40
26  SA, 894/175-177

burgesses of the town (who lost out in the changes) onside by seeming to sympathise with their objections, whilst in reality he was helping to steer through the changes set out in the new constitution of 1582, which took power away from them.

Church records indicate that in 1582 he made a payment to the wardens for a "kneeling place" in the church, and show too that his expertise was often called upon by the church, signing off contracts for building work, counter signing the annual accounts, and in 1601 providing advice in relation to the bitter dispute over the appointment of a new vicar, when the Rev. Nathaniel Tattersall went to court to oust the Rev. Richard Piggott[27]. Mr Yale was a co-defendant with Mr Piggott in that action – which resulted in victory for Mr Tattersall, heralding in ten years of conflict culminating in Tattersall being deprived of the living.

In 1603, Hugh Yale signed the declaration of the burgesses seeking to persuade the earl of Suffolk, who had recently acquired the manorial rights to Oswestry, to protect the town's ancient rights. By this time, he was very much an elder statesman. As such, in 1604, then aged 75, he was called upon to give evidence in a dispute with Thomas Hanmer of Porkington over rights to common land at Cyrn-y-Bwch and Llawnt yr Afon Goch, below what we know as the Racecourse. His evidence is preserved in the Town Council archives; in one extract Mr Yale notes that "David Hanmer gent nowe deceased about three or fower yeres past warned and hind'red some of the inhabitants of Oswestrie from cutting of heath turffe and gorse upon the said mountaine called Kyrne y bwche"[28].

He was not a native of the town; his father was David Lloyd ab Ellis of Plas-yn-Iâl, Denbighshire, where he would have been brought up and educated. However, his mother was Gwenhwyfar, daughter of Richard Lloyd of Llwynymaen and it is very likely that the Yale family's links with Oswestry, and the Yales' property interests in our area began in the 1520s with Gwenhwyfar's marriage to David Lloyd ab Ellis. Hugh Yale was therefore the cousin of both the Lloyds of Llanforda and of the Lloyds of Llwynymaen, whose double-headed eagle symbol can be seen on the side of St Oswald's font and on the Llwyd Mansion. He was one of several sons; his brothers were John Yale, Griffith Lloyd, Thomas Yale and Roger Lloyd (the use of permanent surnames in Wales was in its early days, and not all of Hugh Yale's brothers took the same approach). There were also at least two sisters. Recorded as 75 years old in 1604, Hugh would have been born in 1529 or 1530. He was probably the fourth son.

---

27  National Archives, E112/64/579
28  OTC, A78/2

There is no surviving reference (at least none that I am aware of) to Hugh Yale owning property in Oswestry earlier than 1580. A survey of October 1577 includes no references to him, though it does record that Hugh's elder brother "Tho. Yale Doctor" held two crofts containing 3 acres, formerly belonging to Haughmond Abbey, and also "one Chappell of Oswald and ix closures lyinge together being an hundred acres"[29]. Thomas Yale, doctor of laws, was an important figure in the Anglican church, holding at different times various key roles, during the reigns of both Queen Mary and her sister Queen Elizabeth. He was one of the executors of the will of Archbishop of Canterbury, Matthew Parker, on his death in 1575. Thomas Yale died in November 1577[30]. His will survives, as does that of his widow Joanna who died in 1587[31]. Thomas's will included a bequest to his brother Hugh of his lands in Oswestry, after his wife Joanna's death, for Hugh's life only, so that after Hugh's death, they were to pass to Thomas's rightful heir (the son of his eldest brother John Yale). His brother Roger was the beneficiary of a similarly worded bequest of land at Faenol. Thomas's brothers Hugh and Roger were two of his appointed executors.

Thomas noted that "my mind ys in no ways to have any pompous burial but decent modest with as little cost as may be, being manifestly yt may be better bestowed upon my poore kynsfolks". He also suggested that his wife should, for "most quietness", enter into agreements with his brothers Hugh and Roger "that she may be answered of the rents out of Wales [including in this context Oswestry] here at London": that is, that they should collect the rent on her behalf, avoiding the need for her to travel from her home in the city of London.

Other later rentals of Oswestry show that beyond a life interest in the chapel fields Hugh Yale owned other local property in his own right, including a barn in Church Street, land near Shelf Bank, and other lands in Treflach. In January 1580, he acquired property next to the churchyard, part of which had the name *Bwlen*, purchasing it from the London goldsmith Richard Rogers[32]. In 1606, this property, now described as "my cottage commonly called Bullen" and other adjacent property with the name *y Ty* or *Tythin yn y fynwent* were placed in trust for the benefit of the poor of Oswestry in accordance with instructions in Hugh Yale's will.

---

29  W.J. Slack (ed.), *The lordship of Oswestry, 1393-1607: a series of extents and rentals* (1951), p134
30  *Oxford dictionary of national biography* (2004), 60, p723-724
31  National Archives, PROB 11/60/195, PROB 11/71/292
32  NLW, Aston Hall 960

Turning now to the monument itself, it is perhaps the case that what we see today, setting aside its interesting history, is a little dull – plain, grey stone, with "the big figures, kneeling at a prayer desk, crudely carved" according to the new Pevsner's architectural guide to the buildings of Shropshire. Is this fair? Taking a close look at the figures, armed with a powerful torch, it is clear that the carving is not *that* crude: consider the row of buttons on Hugh's doublet or Dorothy's finely detailed sleeves, or the hassocks on which the couple are kneeling.

We must remember that, in earlier times, the monument was painted, with brightly coloured Corinthian columns and, above the entablature, painted strapwork and the family coat of arms in its heraldic colours. The Yale arms are those on the left-hand side. These show a background of ermine (white, with black 'ermine spots') with a red saltire cross, and at the centre of the cross a yellow or gold crescent – in the terminology of heraldry, "ermine, on a saltire gules, a crescent or". On the right-hand side are the arms of Dorothy Yale's family, the Rodens or Roydens of Burton in the present-day parish of Isycoed, about five miles to the east of Wrexham. Described in heraldic terminology the Royden arms are "azure, three roebucks' heads erased in bend or" – that is, against a background of azure blue, three bucks' heads with jagged or uneven edges (not *couped* or clean cut) in yellow or gold set diagonally from upper left to lower right. Above the shield is the Yale crest, an azure boar within a net coloured yellow or gold, set on a red hat ("chapeau gules") turned up ermine. Black & white photographs from a century ago show that, at that time, the coat of arms was plain and unpainted; the present colour was added about fifty years ago. Examine the figure of Hugh Yale, and you can see traces of old, flesh coloured paint on his fingers and face, of black paint on his gown, of a creamy brown paint for the fur edging to that gown, and of a pinky red paint for the kneelers. In comparison, the figure of Dorothy seems to have lost almost all its paint. It is possible that the paint may have been stripped off at some stage, perhaps accounting for the degraded features of Dorothy's face and hands. In its original state, the monument would have been eye-catching, in the way that newly restored, repainted and regilded Tudor and Jacobean monuments are sometimes to be seen in cathedrals and churches today.

The Yale monument. A coloured drawing from the papers of the antiquarian William Mytton, Mytton Papers MYT/5/988. © Cadbury Research Library, University of Birmingham. Reproduced with permission.

The inscription is currently very difficult to make out, and what is, barely, readable from ground level shows that the lettering has been re-applied at least once before: one short phrase ('in the late warrs An'o 1616') can be seen both on the left-hand side and in a slightly different script just to the right side of the arch. The wording of the inscription is known – it has been recorded a number of times down the years – in the early 18th century Mytton Papers[33], in Price's *History* (1815), by Stanley Leighton in 1874, and by John Askew Roberts in 1880.

William Mytton recorded the text as follows: "In memorie of Mr Hugh Yale Alderman of this Town and Dorothy his wife daughter of Roger Rhod- [Royden] of Burton in the county of Denbigh Esq. whose bodies are interred within the chancell of this church commonly called St Marie's before its demolition in the late warrs An'o 1616. They gave to the poor of this Town the yearly interest & benefit of one hundred pounds to continue forever besides many other good actes of Charitie".

The reference to the Civil War – 'the late wars' – shows that the inscription was added at the time of the restoration of the church, when the monument was moved from the north chancel to its present location in the north aisle. The date 1616 is a puzzle – is it a mistake, the result of a misreading of the date 1676 when lettering was being renewed at some point? Or does it relate to the date that the monument was first erected? We know that Hugh Yale died in January 1606, and it seems likely that Dorothy died in 1610 or 1611 – but it is possible that their executors were a little tardy in commissioning a monument.

Finally, there is the marble mural tablet set behind the two figures. Added in the mid-eighteenth century, this commemorates David Yale Esq., of Plas-yn-lâl (d. 1763) and his wife Margaret (d. 1754), who had lived in Church Street, and whose remains lie beneath the monument. Whilst this later tablet may seem something of an interloper, something that detracts from the Renaissance lines of the Jacobean monument, it serves to remind us that the Yale monument, when newly erected, may well have included a *carved* inscription, immediately below the two kneeling figures, or behind them in the place now occupied by the later tablet, that was lost during the destruction of the Civil War, or when the monument was moved to its present location in the late 17th century. Likewise, the monument would have been one of a number of impressive Tudor and Jacobean memorials in the pre-Civil War church.

*Based on articles printed in St Oswald's Parish Magazine for January, February and March 2016 and May 2017*

---

33  University of Birmingham, Cadbury Research Library, Mytton Papers, MYT/5/988-989

# Chapter 11: An investigation of Corporation malpractice

St Oswald's has had close links with Oswestry School from the very start, from the establishment of the school in the early years of the 15th century by David Holbache and his wife Gwenhwyfar. The then vicar of Oswestry, Richard Hova, was one of nineteen foundation trustees of the school.

The school was maintained by a portfolio of endowments, principally by lands and property in Oswestry and district which had been given by David Holbache for this purpose, which supplemented the pupils' fees. The school's properties were leased out, with the rents providing income for the school. In addition, some of the land was wooded, providing both a ready supply of timber for building maintenance work on the half-timbered school house which stood next to the churchyard, and an additional source of income from the sale of surplus timber.

By Tudor times, the administration of the school lands was in the hands of the Corporation, with the leading role taken by the two bailiffs, elected each year by the common council of Oswestry. A document of 1538 indicated that the bailiffs, and the aldermen of the town "shall have the ordering, letting and setting [of] all the lands, tenements and mills … and … see the rents and profitts thereof levied … and bestowed" towards the keeping of a free school, including fees due to the schoolmaster and his assistant (known as an usher). Another document, of 1577, shows that the vicar of St Oswald's also played a role, alongside the bailiffs, in the governance of the school[34].

A document of 1613 seems to suggest that good governance was being maintained, recording a decision made by the council, with the consent of the schoolmaster, "that the woodes growing upon the Schoole lands shall be sould to the best pryse by the nowe Bailiffs" in order to pay for the maintenance of an usher, the agreement also noting that "two hundred trees selected by the Bailiffs & their associats be preserved for the best use of the schoole & towards the continuall reparacon of the same"[35].

---

34 A. Roberts, 'Oswestry Grammar School', *Trans. Shrops. Arch. Soc.*, 5 (1882), p5-10
35 A. Roberts, 'Oswestry Grammar School', *Trans. Shrops. Arch. Soc.*, 5 (1882), p16-17

However, this agreement masked the true position, which only emerged twenty years later when the bishop of St Asaph was invited in, possibly at the request of the vicar John Kyffin, to investigate malpractice over many years by the bailiffs. The commission of enquiry, which included the bishop and his chancellor William Griffith, doctor of law, and several other senior figures, met at Oswestry on September 17th 1634[36].

Evidence was presented indicating that leases had been granted following cash payments to Dorothy Cowper and Katherine Blodwell, the wives of the bailiffs William Cowper and Henry Blodwell, "by way of gratuity and reward for the procuring of [their husbands] to join in making leases". Other evidence showed that William Heilyn and William Morris, the bailiffs for 1611, had sold crops of trees worth ten pounds "and received the Ten Pounds but neither paid nor employed the same at all to the use of the Schoolmaster or Schoolhouse". Several other bailiffs were accused of the same offence, in other years, so that it was found "some of the best timber trees are made away, and not employed to the use of the School, neither any account or recompence have been made".

In a highly critical judgment, the commissioners ruled that the bailiffs and their successors should be discharged as trustees for the school. Responsibility for selecting the schoolmaster would in future be left to the bishop of St Asaph, whilst the schoolmaster was given charge of letting out the school lands, with his recommendations ratified by the bishop and chancellor as well as the bailiffs, or by two of them - one of whom had to be the bishop. Decisions to cut down trees likewise needed the consent of bishop, chancellor and bailiffs.

Edward Payne, then the schoolmaster, was required to undertake, within the year, a detailed survey of the school lands "together with the number of timber trees thereupon". He was instructed to provide one copy to the corporation and the other to the bishop. Completed in 1635, the bishop's copy survives; it is preserved amongst the Lichfield Diocesan archives[37].

*Based on an article printed in St Oswald's Parish Magazine for December 2015*

---

36  Ibid., p17-29
37  Now held at Staffordshire Record Office

## Chapter 12: From Middleton to Aleppo – tales of a Turkey merchant

We sometimes assume that in the days before the invention of the train, the car and the aeroplane, when travel was on foot or restricted to horse power, people generally stayed close to home. We assume that in Tudor times, most local people travelled no further than from, say, Trefonen into Oswestry, perhaps for the market, with a trip to Shrewsbury a rare adventure, and travel beyond the county town seen as a journey to the other side of the world.

Historical records show that, of course, many local people did stay put, and travel between Shrewsbury and Oswestry in the time of Elizabeth Tudor was indeed an adventure, with Shrewsbury merchants worried about attacks by thieves and highwaymen on the journey. However, it is surprising to find just how far some Oswestrians did manage to travel, four hundred years ago.

Take for example John Davies, who lived in Middleton in the second half of the sixteenth century. Born in around 1565, he died in 1636. His family could trace their descent back to the fourteenth century, his ancestors living in Dudleston and then in Middleton. Like his father before him he had gradually expanded the family's possessions - their lands and property in Middleton, and in Oswestry – and had achieved a position of influence and some status in Oswestry. He was a churchwarden for St Oswald's in 1594; he was one of the jurors appointed to a commission established in 1602 to assist in a survey of the lordship of Oswestry for the earl of Suffolk (so that the earl could exploit his new assets to the full), and in 1606 he was high constable of the Hundred of Oswestry, responsible for collecting money due to the poor and sick. In 1598 he had paid forty shillings for a kneeling place in a prominent place in the parish church.

John Davies and his wife Elizabeth had six sons and four daughters, each baptised at St Oswald's between 1589 and 1606. Oswestry's historians down the years, and students of Oswestry's history, will be familiar with the eldest son, another John Davies, born in 1589: he was the author and compiler of an important handwritten history of Oswestry, and of the barony of Oswestry, completed in 1635, and preserved in the British Library. This had been commissioned by the earl of Arundel when he had visited Oswestry in 1629 or 1630. John Davies, the son, had trained as a lawyer, being admitted to Lincoln's Inn off Chancery Lane in central London in 1612 as "John Davis, gent., son of John Davis of Middleton, gent." being called to the bar seven years later. It seems likely that he practised in London until the mid-1620s, before returning to live at the family home in Middleton. He was married in 1618, his bride being Elizabeth Pudsey, the daughter of another lawyer, originally from Yorkshire, their wedding taking place at St Margaret's, Westminster, the parish church located next to Westminster Abbey and close to Westminster Hall. After his return to Oswestry, he was appointed Recorder for the borough and corporation: the town's royal charter of 1617 had noted that "there may and shalbe one honest and discreet man which shalbe learned in the lawes of England which shall and may be the recorder of the Borough and shalbe soe called"[38].

At least three of John's brothers, Richard, Thomas and Daniel, followed him to London. In details provided by Richard Davies to the college of heralds in 1633, Richard describes himself as formerly the "esquire of the body extraordinary to King James" and as a "merchant of London", listing his brother Thomas Davies as a merchant, and his brother Daniel as a grocer. It seems that all three brothers were apprenticed to members of the livery companies in London. The cost of these apprenticeships, and the significant expense of John's legal training, represents a massive investment by their father, explaining why he was selling some of his property, and mortgaging others, in Oswestry in 1609.

Our present focus is on the third son, Thomas Davies, baptised at St Oswald's on October 20th 1593 as "Thomas ap John Dd of Mydelton". His story shows us just how far someone could travel, how much someone could achieve, and in what circles they could move, at this time. Born and brought up in Middleton and in Oswestry, by the age of 30, in 1624, Thomas was living in Aleppo, in Syria, in what was then part of the Turkish Ottoman Empire.

---

38  J. Pryce-Jones, 'John Davies of Middleton, an early Shropshire historian', *Trans. Shrops. Arch. & Hist. Soc.*, 75 (2000), p85-102

What exactly was Thomas Davies doing in the Middle East, so far from his roots on the Welsh border?  Thomas was the Factor General for the Levant Company, generally known at the time as the Turkey Merchants, resident at their base in Aleppo, at the western end of the Silk Road.  A history of the company has described Aleppo as "the entrepôt for eastern goods brought overland by the caravan routes from the Euphrates and the Persian Gulf", with its importance as a trading base equal to that of Constantinople, modern day Istanbul.   The Levant Company had been established by royal charter in 1581, when it was granted a monopoly of the English (and Welsh) trade with the immense Turkish Empire.  The company bought Persian silks, oriental goods and spices, for onward sale in London, and also cotton wool, sent back to England to be made into fustian cloth in Bolton and Manchester.  In return the company sold English cloth, as well as tin, lead and furs to the Turks.  It is interesting to note, from surviving accounts of 1630 and 1631 preserved in the archives of the University of London[39], that Thomas Davies was working closely in this trade with his brother Richard – the documents show that Richard Davies was sending broadcloth out to his brother in Aleppo, and Thomas was sending Richard supplies of fine silk in return.  This in itself is interesting – it's amazing to think of two boys, brought up in Oswestry in the 1590s, quite probably educated at the free school next to the parish church, working in this way, corresponding with one another by letter, and with their goods conveyed by trading vessels sailing between London and Antioch on the Mediterranean coast.

But this was just part of it, and perhaps less significant than Thomas Davies' other role whilst at Aleppo.  The presence of the Levant Company and of resident English merchants in the Near East – often living in the area for many years – was an ideal way of obtaining old documents – both originals and commissioned copies – to assist Tudor and Stuart scholars in their studies of the Bible, the Holy Land, and the Arab world.  The historian C.E. Bosworth, in the book *Mapping Islamic studies* (1997) noted that "Levant Company merchants were commissioned to obtain Arabic, Persian, Turkish, Syriac, Hebrew and Samaritan manuscripts".  This was a boon to Bible scholars such as Archbishop William Laud who, in 1634, obtained rights from king Charles I requiring every ship of the Levant Company on each journey back to England from the East to bring back one Arabic or Persian manuscript for him.

---

39    University of London, Senate House Library, GB96, ms655

Aleppo sat at the cross roads, ideally placed for this research, and letters[40] from 1624 to 1628 survive which show the important role played by Thomas Davies. He had been engaged by James Ussher, bishop of Meath and from 1625 archbishop of Armagh, to locate, purchase and send back ancient texts to him. In these letters, Thomas described in some detail the actions he was taking to obtain these documents. In 1624, he wrote to the bishop that he had found a Samaritan Old Testament, which he reported was slightly imperfect, "which notwithstanding I purpose to send by this shipp least I meet not with another". He had sent to Damascus for a perfect Pentateuch, and had sent a messenger to Mount Lebanon and Tripoli for a Syriac Old Testament but without success. He had been offered a Hebrew version, he said, for the princely sum of £10, but could not guarantee it "for neyther my selfe nor any other man here can determine it, only I must be forced to take his word that sells it me who is a minister of the sect of the Marranites". He noted somewhat ruefully that "to affect business of this nature in these parts requires time, travel being very tedious in these countries".

In another letter, of January 1626, he described how he had sent to Damascus "to see if I could procure the Grammar, Chronicles and Calendar which your Lordship desires, but could not obtain any of them, there being but one poor man of the Samaritan race left in Damascus, who is not able to satisfy me in any thing you desire only he said there were certain Books in their language pawned to a great Spahee of that City but what they contained the poor fellow knew not. The Spahee would not part with them under 200 Dollars which is 60 pounds sterling".

Again, Thomas Davies wrote that "From Emmit [Amid, modern day Diyarbakir in south eastern Turkey] I hope to have some good News to write your Lordship, and to send you a Catalogue of such Books as be here to be had. When this book which I now send shall be received, I beseech your Grace to give your secretary order to advise me thereof; in the meantime, if any of the Books you desire shall be brought or sent unto me, I will not let them go for a small matter or less: such Books are very rare, and esteemed as Jewels by the Owners, tho' they know not how to use them, neither will they part with them but at dear rates, especially to Strangers who they presume would not seek after them except they were of good worth".

---

40 R. Parr (ed.), *The life of the most reverend father in God James Ussher ... with a collection of three hundred letters* (1686), p311-313, 323-327, 371-372, 381-382; C.R. Elrington & J.H. Todd, *The whole works of ... James Ussher* (1847-64), 16, p444-445, 472-473

James Ussher, Archbishop of Armagh, for whom Thomas Davies obtained numerous early documents. © National Portrait Gallery, London. Reproduced with permission.

Thomas Davies' bills were settled by payment made to his brother Richard; in July 1628 he wrote to the archbishop, "here inclosed a note of the books sent per [the ship *Hercules* of London] with the cost and charges thereof, and of them sent last, amounting to the sum of thirty nine pounds eighteen shillings which I pray may be paid to my brother Richard Davis or to whom he shall order it".

James Ussher is perhaps best known today as the theologian whose studies enabled him to answer what has been described as "the great theological and cosmological question of the day – the precise date of the foundation of the world". He achieved this by many years of Bible study which allowed him to produce a detailed chronology of events which linked biblical and ancient history, declaring October 23rd in the year 4004 B.C. to be the sought for date. The books and manuscripts provided by Thomas Davies contributed to Ussher's studies, but in addition the archbishop encouraged Davies to make other enquiries on his behalf, for instance relating to a note in the Old Testament Book of Joshua to the river Jordan that it "overflows all its banks throughout the time of harvest". In a letter dated August 29th 1624, Thomas Davies wrote "I have inquired of divers, both Christians and Jews, of the overflowing of Jordan, but can learn no certainty. Some say it never rises but after great Rain, but I met a learned Jew (at least so reputed) who told me that Jordan begins to flow the 13th of July, and continues flowing 29 days, and is some 18 or 20 days increasing: but I dare not believe him, his relation not agreeing with the text, for Harvest is near ended with them by that time, and unless you will understand by Harvest the time of gathering grapes, it cannot agree".

It is also interesting to note that Thomas Davies also provided James Ussher with a commentary on current affairs in the Near East where, at that time, the Ottoman rulers of Turkey were at war with the Persians, and at the same time were seeking to deal with a rebellion amongst their own forces. For example, in July 1625, Davies reported that "the Turks Forces were before Bagdat, and during the Siege the Persians sallied out of the City divers times and had many Skirmishes with the Turks, but ever came off with Honour, and slew the Turks in great numbers, who after eight Months were forced to raise their Siege and be gone". Thomas clearly had to be adept in the diplomatic arts, and to be able to negotiate the various local and international rivalries that existed in his world in Aleppo – in July 1628 he complained to the archbishop that "in the road to Scanderon some English under command of Sir Kenelm Digby have made such a fight with French and Venetians that hath cost the merchants fourteen thousand pounds besides the dishonour the nation have received by the imprisonment of our consul". He added, with feeling, "Patience, we are in Turkey, God bring us out of it; we are enclosed with our enemies, not only Turks and Jews, but the French and false Venetians labour our ruin. But I trust God is on our side, and will not suffer us to be swallowed up of inveterate malice".

It's still a very long way from Oswestry to Aleppo. How much further away must Aleppo have felt back in the 1620s and 1630s? Surviving documents show that Thomas Davies was based in Aleppo from at least 1624 to 1633, by which date he would have reached the age of 40. He was able to correspond, with his relations and with clients such as James Ussher back in the British Isles, by letter, sent by ship, though each letter took several months to arrive: in a letter of November 14th 1626, Thomas wrote that he had just received the archbishop of Armagh's letter of July 31st, in which the cleric noted receipt of Thomas's letter of January 16th. It is clear that Thomas thought of his family back at home: in a letter of March 1627, he thanked the archbishop "for the favours you conferred upon my poor sister" (he does not say which one) and ends the letter with a somewhat poignant postscript "I pray commend me to my sister, and if married to her husband".

Whether Thomas Davies ever returned home is not known, but it is quite likely that he died in Syria. It was the case that although the trade offered Turkey Merchants the prospect of immense riches, the traders' survival was very uncertain with hot summers, crowded towns and cities, and with traders passing through Aleppo from many other places, making illness and contagion a constant risk. Tellingly, a traveller writing in 1596 had commented that few company factors returned alive from Aleppo.

*Based on an article printed in St Oswald's Parish Magazine for April 2013, subsequently reprinted in an expanded form in the Oswestry Advertizer for June 14th and 21st 2016*

# Chapter 13: The importance of wool and leather to Oswestry's economy - evidence from the parish registers

Parish registers are a very valuable source of information for the local historian. Oswestry's registers survive from November 1558, with only a small number of short gaps, and unlike many other early records they cover the whole spread of the local community: rich and poor, landed and landless, men, women and children. Whilst the purpose of these register entries was simply to record baptisms, marriages and burials, day by day, month by month, in the parish, they can often provide the local historian with other useful information including family relationships, where people lived, and their occupations. An analysis of Oswestry's registers, focussing on a series of four ten year spans, starting with the years 1615 to 1624, and repeating the exercise at fifty year intervals, for the years 1665 to 1674, then 1715 to 1724, through to 1765 to 1774, has provided a valuable insight into local trades and occupations, and an indication as to changing times, changing fashions and how the local economy adapted to these changes.

It has also shown how some trades gravitated to a particular street or area of the town. For instance, this analysis has revealed how, in the years 1665 to 1674, Oswestry's butchers' shops were concentrated in one street, namely Cross Street, which at that time ran between the Cross and the New Gate. Twenty nine individuals are described as butchers in the registers for those ten years; the addresses of sixteen of those men are listed in the registers, and of them fourteen lived in Cross Street. It is known that, in mediaeval towns, trades would often be grouped together, sometimes with a street name indicative of that trade – Butcher Row and Fish Street in Shrewsbury are good examples. The choice of Cross Street as the focus for Oswestry's butchers' premises was a sound one, reflecting the lie of the land, and the gradual slope from the top of Willow Street, and from the Bailey Head, down to the Cross, and on towards Roft Street and Salop Road. A number of streams run down through the town from the adjacent hills, so that waste or pollution from the butchers' premises in Cross Street, particularly those whose properties backed on to the town walls, would have flowed straight out of the town into the ditch of the town walls (the present English Walls) and away towards the river Morda.

Various local trades would have been dirty and smelly – tanning being a prime example. In 1631 Edward Edwards, a local tanner, donated a silver cup and plate to St Oswald's[41]; it is known that his tannery was located in Church Street, and it is to be hoped that his tanning works were sited downwind of the church. That said, it may be that in earlier centuries people just accepted these smells, and the nuisance arising from such trades, as the way of the world. Certainly, the analysis of local parish registers makes clear just how many local families depended on the leather trade at this time, and highlights that, although the wool trade and Oswestry's position as the market place where Welsh weavers sold their wares to the rich drapers from Shrewsbury, were critical to the local economy, it was not the only important trade in the town. Indeed, the most common single occupation recorded in the register for the years 1615 to 1624 was not part of the wool trade at all – rather it was that of the corviser, or shoemaker, with sixty nine parishioners[42] so described. Taken together, there were one hundred and thirty five men listed whose occupations placed them in the wool or cloth trade, including sixty one weavers, forty six shearmen, twelve mercers, as well as drapers, dyers, hatmakers, and walkers (fullers). A further nine weavers were listed in the rural parts of the parish, in Maesbury, Trefonen, Sweeney and Morton. Matching this were one hundred and twenty seven parishioners listed whose occupations placed them in the leather trade: the aforesaid shoemakers, plus forty four glovers, four tanners, five curriers, and two skinners. In direct employment terms it is clear that leather was of equal importance to the wool trade in Oswestry at this time, something which has largely gone unrecognised.

---

41  A church inventory of 1791 recorded the inscription on a silver chalice and paten "Edward Edwards Tanner dedicateth this Plate to the Service of God in the church of Oswestrie the chardge beinge his Friends love at the Baptisme of Francis and Catharine his childrine now both with God. 1631"
42  In addition, there were two men described in the register as cobblers

That said, historians have described the loss of the weekly wool market to Shrewsbury in the 1620s as a body blow to the town. The loss of the business brought into the town each Monday, the buying and selling of woollen cloth in the streets and in inns and public houses was indeed a severe blow to the prosperity of the town, followed twenty years later by the destruction caused in the Civil War, but parish registers for 1665 to 1674 show that the woollen industry remained important to Oswestry with thirty five weavers listed in the town plus another sixteen in the rural districts, twenty five tailors plus ten more in the rural parts, twenty three shearmen and clothworkers, and nine men working as hat makers or felt makers. That said, the number of people working in the leather trades had now overtaken that for the cloth trade – with forty seven corvisers[43], thirty five glovers plus another nine in the rural parts, seven tanners with five more in the countryside, four curriers, along with a specialist bridle maker and four saddlers. It is interesting to note that the Morda valley was becoming a focus for those aspects of both trades that required running water: for example, whilst the ten-year sample found no dyers in the town of Oswestry, there were five in the rural townships, in Weston, Llanforda and Pentreshannel, and likewise the only two fullers found in this sample were based in Sweeney and Llanforda. In addition, there were twenty one men listed in this sample as colliers, in Trefonen, Treflach, Trefarclawdd, Pentreshannel, Gronwen and Sweeney, with another five living in the town.

By the early years of the 18th century, evidence from the third ten year sample, for the years 1715 to 1724, indicates how the number working in the leather industries was still significant, with forty three corvisers in town and country, and thirty five glovers, and others described as skinners, tanners and saddlers. By contrast, the number engaged in the cloth trade had fallen back, with only seventeen weavers and twenty six tailors among the sample. Move forward another fifty years and the picture changes again: whilst the number employed as weavers and tailors has remained much the same, the number working as glovers has plummeted to just nine, and the number of shoemakers has fallen to twenty four.

---

43   There were two more in the rural townships

Turning to other trades, it is noticeable that although the early registers include numerous references to blacksmiths, there are surprisingly few indications of other metal-based trades, to the making of cooking pots, plates and cutlery, or to gold and silver jewellery.  Where did local people go?  Were their needs met by the blacksmith?  Did the more affluent buy from Shrewsbury or Chester?  Or were these goods that were purchased from itinerant merchants or makers at the weekly market, or at the seasonal fairs?  Clearly these goods were to be found in local homes as they are often mentioned in wills of the time; for instance, the will of Edward Baker (1608) included a bequest of twelve silver spoons stored in the parlour cupboard in his house in Middle Street.  The ten-year sample of the registers, for the years 1615 to 1624, included very few local tradesmen seeking to satisfy local demand – the aforementioned Edward Baker was a pewterer; John Woods (d. 1615) of Leg Street was a cutler; and David ap Richard, mentioned in 1619, was a brazier, making domestic ware in brass.

Over the next fifty years, the range of occupations increased, with greater specialisation both in making and in selling.  Restoration Oswestry had a resident cutler Richard Tyser of Leg Street, and a button maker, William Lloyd, as well as an oatmeal seller Hugh ap Edward ap Evan, a cheesemonger Evan Jones of Willow Street, and two ironmongers.  By the close of the 17th century, the registers provide evidence of increasing specialisation, with parishioners described as gunsmiths, plasterers, tobacco sellers, pipe makers and chimney sweeps.  As the 18th century progressed, the town had its own breeches makers, stays makers and hosiers.  Changing fashion had already introduced the trade of peruke or periwig making to the town: the registers include references to John Jennings of Cross Street, in 1688, and to Thomas Talbot, also of Cross Street, in 1691, both described as perwick makers, and the churchwarden Peter Povall, whose name can be found engraved over the now blocked up north door to St Oswald's, dated 1715, was another wig maker.  As the 18th century progressed, the range of goods, and the range of trades continued to grow: the sample for the years 1765 to 1774 included three clockmakers, John Gardner and Joseph Salter in Oswestry, and Edward Francis in Maesbury[44].

---

[44] The earliest register entry to a local clock or watch maker (Charles Wicksteed) dates from 1730

Coal mining continued to be important to the local economy. It is interesting to note that the third sample, for the years 1715 to 1724 shows a slight reduction in the number of parishioners listed in the register as 'collier', with only three men from the town, and seven from the rural townships of Sweeney, Trefonen and Trefarclawdd. However, fifty years on, the final sample, for 1765 to 1774, includes twenty seven colliers in the rural townships, from Maesbury through to Llanforda and Pentreshannel, and a further eighteen living in Oswestry, plus a coal carrier, William Hughes of Trefonen, and Mr Thomas, described in 1771 as steward of the coal works at Gronwen.

Finally, what about light entertainment? References in the registers to harpers, David Davies (1658) and Moris Rynalds of the Three Tuns (1691), and to fiddlers Thomas and Richard Hughes in the 1720s and 1730s, shed a small amount of light on local society, though it is not clear whether these men simply played to audiences in local taverns or entertained the local gentry – perhaps they did both. There are also various references to David Evans of Llanforda (d. 1711), described as the blind fiddler. Eyton Johnson, listed in 1745, was described as a dancing master. It is known that there was a theatre in Oswestry from 1775 or earlier. Initially this was located in Lower Brook Street and then, from 1819, in Willow Street. Companies of actors travelled from place to place, performing at assembly halls or the houses of gentry: the registers for 1728 refer to the showman Isaac Birch of Newport, those for 1746 list the baptism of a daughter of John Ward, "one of the Comedian Band of St Austin, Middlesex" and, in 1775, the son of Thomas Phillips, comedian, was baptised, the register noting that he had been born at Mr Rathbone's in Cross Street. Charles Stanton, proprietor of the Oswestry Theatre, also took his players on tour – and St Oswald's registers for 1812 record the baptism of two of his children, Emily and Francis, born 'on the road', in Nantwich and Stafford.

*Based partly on articles printed in St Oswald's Parish Magazine for July and August 2010*

## Chapter 14: Solving a mystery in the parish church

The triptych, or the reredos, featuring Moses and Aaron, which is to be found high on the south wall of the Lady Chapel of Oswestry parish church is a remarkable and an eye-catching object, which was brought back to life by its restoration by Hirst Conservation in 2004, and provides a reminder of the church before G.E. Street's restorations of 1872/74. In the recent revised and expanded Shropshire volume (2006) of the *Buildings of England* series of books it is described as "an exceptionally fine early 18$^{th}$ century triptych of Creed, Lord's Prayer and Decalogue ... in the centre, full length figures of Moses and Aaron hold the Tablets of the Law, with radiant name of God above". In the original 1958 edition, by Sir Nikolaus Pevsner, it was not mentioned at all; neither did it merit a reference in the detailed description of St Oswald's in the Rev. D.H.S. Cranage's multi-volume *Architectural account of the churches of Shropshire* (1894-1912). It is likely that both omissions were for the simple reason that the triptych was hidden away in the tower, fixed to an inside wall, having been moved there shortly before Street's time when the present east window was installed.

Prior to that time, it had stood – or was affixed – immediately behind the altar as a reredos or altarpiece. Askew Roberts, writing in 1881, recalled that "the east window of the chancel was filled up by painted boards containing the Ten Commandments, flanked on either side by Gog and Magog-like painted figures which were supposed to represent Moses and Aaron"; Mr Roberts added that the boards "disfigured the east window". There is a further description of the chancel, from Thomas Martyn, a visitor from London, in August 1801. In his travel diary, he noted that above the altar and below the east window were "whole length figures of Moses and Aaron, with the Tablets containing the Decalogue between them, on one side the Lord's Prayer and on the other the Apostles' Creed". He also described the window behind: it was "lofty, with angels sounding their trumpets" adding that it was "tolerably well painted" – rare evidence that there was decorative glass in the pre-Victorian St Oswald's.

The Moses and Aaron triptych, displayed on the south wall of the Lady Chapel in St Oswald's parish church. Photograph © John Pryce-Jones.

The triptych is not unique – there are other similar examples in various parts of the country. There is an example in Llansilin parish church. However, it is a comparatively rare survival of something that was, in the late 17th and the 18th century, a common addition to parish churches. Academic studies have pointed out that the use of Moses and Aaron in this manner can be traced back to the frontispiece of the King James Bible.

Turning then to the date of the reredos, the church website suggests that it may date back to before 1730. The churchwardens' accounts for most of the 17th century have not survived, and, with the exception of the period 1579-1615, now begin in 1717. This is a very lucky chance as, in the accounts of Nathaniel Price and Humphrey Kynaston, the churchwardens for the town for both 1717 and 1718, there is listed a payment of nine pounds and fourteen shillings "to Mr Downes of Whitechurch" then unpaid for "the Altar Piece". The reference to the account being unpaid suggests that the cost may well have been incurred by the wardens for the previous year, 1716. Along with the new church bells, installed in 1717, the new reredos seems to represent the final phase of the restoration of the church after the immense damage caused in the Civil War. Interestingly a further, much smaller payment of seventeen shillings and sixpence was paid in 1744 to "Mr Downs for adorning the Altar Piece" – perhaps a payment for minor restoration work at that time.

Other research has confirmed that John Downes, painter, of Whitchurch carried out work in a number of parish churches including Hanmer and Malpas: in 1718, the churchwardens at Malpas paid him £14 for painting the King's Arms and the Commandments in their church. He was the eldest son of another John Downes, a glazier, who died in 1729. John Downes junior was born in the late 1680s; he appears to have lived in Whitchurch all his life and died there in 1757. In 1724, he produced for sale a view of the new St Alkmund's parish church, Whitchurch, which had been completely rebuilt in 1712. His son Bernard Downes was a portrait painter, based in London.

*Based on an article printed in St Oswald's Parish Magazine for December 2016*

## Chapter 15: Playing host to the redcoats

We tend to think of military barracks, and army camps along the lines of the former Park Hall Camp, as the norm in terms of military accommodation in the United Kingdom, with permanent barracks for the local regiment set up in county towns, and with larger scale facilities at towns such as Aldershot. This has been the case, to a greater or lesser extent (allowing for the reduction in the number of regiments, and the merger of many county regiments) for the past two hundred years. However, before that time, things were very different.

Historically, Parliament had always been very wary of having a 'standing army', preferring to raise troops only when the need arose. After the restoration of Charles II, and particularly after the accession of William and Mary, with a Jacobite pretender in the wings, the need for troops to be available on call was recognised and accepted; the series of wars, mainly against France and Spain, at the start of the 18$^{th}$ century, was another factor. However, the country was not yet ready for permanent barracks. Instead soldiers were mostly accommodated in temporary camps or in billets, in private houses or in inns and taverns, always on the move, their regiments constantly travelling around the country. Especially in peacetime, having a body of troops lodged together *en masse* was seen as dangerous, whereas billeting was felt to act as a check on the army, with troops less likely to become estranged from the people as they were in daily close contact with them.

Throughout the 18$^{th}$ century, local parish registers include references to parishioners who had enlisted, such as in October 1757, where the register lists the baptism of John, son of John Jones "gone for a soldier" and Sarah his wife. These though are very occasional references, one every couple of years. There is a small increase for the years 1728 to 1733, with eight references to soldiers, but the presence of eighteen register entries between June 2$^{nd}$ 1734 and April 13$^{th}$ 1735 suggests that Oswestry must have played host to at least part of a regiment at that time.

All but one of these eighteen entries are for baptisms, such as that for October 12th 1734, the baptism of Abraham, son of Matthew Whitworth, a soldier, and Ann, indicating that many of these troops were accompanied in Oswestry by their wives. Also, the names of the soldiers – Burnet, Butt, Dolman, Hastings, Cozens, Howard, French, Fletcher, Chetman and Young – show clearly that the troops were not local men. One entry, that for July 19th 1734, helpfully provides the identity of the regiment that was billeted in Oswestry, recording as it does the christening of Alexander, son of James Hastings, sergeant of Lieutenant General Tatton's Regiment of Foot. At this time military units were often known by the name of their commanding officer, in this case William Tatton, who had been appointed colonel in November 1729. General Tatton's was the 3rd Regiment of Foot, known as the Buffs because of the colour of their jackets, and was later to become the Royal East Kent Regiment.

This is an example of how our parish registers are a valuable source of information about a wide range of local topics, useful to identify short-lived or transitory episodes and incidents which, in times before the arrival of a local newspaper, would otherwise be lost to history. We may have no means of establishing exactly why General Tatton chose to visit Oswestry at this time, or what his troops did whilst they were here, and where they stayed during their stay, but we can imagine the impact that these soldiers had on the life of the town. We can gain something by thinking of Jane Austen's *Pride and prejudice* where the presence of the local militia so enlivened the social life in Meryton, at least for the social elite. No doubt a similar impact would have been felt in Oswestry, in local society circles, as well as in the taverns and on the streets.

*Based on an article printed in St Oswald's Parish Magazine for January 2015*

## Chapter 16: Giving our children a name

It is always interesting to learn from the newspaper, television, or the internet of the names that are chosen by new parents, locally and nationally, which names are the most popular, and which names are no longer as popular as they used to be. The range of names continues to expand, with families able to refer to books of names, and to material on the internet, or to choose names made popular on TV or in films. Parents may elect to give their children names which have a history in their family: for example, a baby might be given the names of its grandparents. In many cases, the choice of names can be a real challenge, something where careful diplomacy may be required to avoid upsetting friends or family who may feel overlooked when one name is selected and others passed over.

That said, the task of selecting our offspring's names is something that today's parents share with parents of previous generations, and, locally, we are fortunate that we have the parish registers, from the mid-16th century onwards, to utilise, to help us to identify patterns and trends in naming over the centuries. In this chapter, the baptism records for St Oswald's have been examined for each of the years 1580, 1680, 1780 and 1880, to see what they can tell us.

During the year 1580 – January to December – there were one hundred and twenty two baptisms at St Oswald's. Of the sixty baby boys baptised, more than half were given one of three names, Richard (15), John (11) or Thomas (7), with other popular names being Robert and Roger (four of each), Morris, Gruffudd and Ieuan (three of each). Of the girls, the most popular name was, unsurprisingly, Elizabeth (10), closely followed by Elinor (9), Anne (7), Katherine and Margaret (both six), and the Welsh names Dowlse (5) and Lowri (4). It is interesting to note that no local boys were given the name Henry in 1580 – and in fact there were only four boys baptised with the name Henry at St Oswald's from the start of the registers in 1558 to the end of the 16th century. Likewise, only one girl was given the name Mary in 1580, though the name gradually regained popularity later in the 1580s and 1590s.

In 1680, a century later, the number of baptisms was very similar (126). Elizabeth remained the most popular of the girls' names (11), followed by Anne (8) and a resurgent Mary (8), Jane (6), Katherine (5), and by Margaret and Sarah (four of each). No children were baptised Elinor or any of its variations in the year 1680, though the name had not entirely fallen from favour as there were ten Elinors baptised at St Oswald's during the ten years of the 1680s. Turning to the boys, John was now the most popular name (14), with Edward (12) next, followed by Richard (8), Thomas (5) and Robert (4). Twenty years on from the Restoration, and the upheaval of the Civil War, there was just the one Charles, and no babies given the name Oliver. That said, looking at a broader spread of years, we see that the name Charles first appeared in our registers in 1630, with a noticeable increase in the name's use in the 1670s and 1680s.

Moving on again, to 1780, there was a smaller number of baptisms at St Oswald's, one hundred and one, and a marked difference between the number of boys (60) and girls (41) baptised. The range of girls' names was notably small – only ten different names overall – with Mary now the most popular (10), followed by Sarah (8) and Ann, now largely without a final letter 'e' (7). Elizabeth had slipped back to four, and Catherine (now spelled with a 'c') to just two. John remained top of the boys' names table with seventeen examples, followed by Thomas (10), Richard (7) and Edward (6).

Finally, in 1880, there were ninety seven baptisms at St Oswald's. In previous centuries, no children had received more than the one Christian name; however, in 1880, almost two-thirds had two or more first names. Most middle names were simply additional forenames (e.g. Margaret Ann Morris, baptised in January 1880) though others had middle names which appear to have been family names (e.g. Kathleen Mackenzie Bull, baptised in August 1880). With so many names required, particularly with large families, the range of different names in the sample, seventy eight in all, was more than double that of previous centuries – including names such as Violet, Ethel, Cecil and Alfred. Of the girls' names, Mary (11) and Ann/Annie (10) remained most popular, with Sarah (6), Margaret (5), and Jane, Alice, Emma and Edith (four each) next. Of the boys' names, George (8) was now most numerous, followed by William (7), and Henry, John, Herbert and Albert (five each). Albert of course was a new arrival – first featuring in Oswestry's baptism registers in 1824, it became a popular choice after Prince Albert's death in 1861. Similarly, the forename Gordon entered our registers in 1884, prompted no doubt by the press coverage of the failed attempt to rescue General Gordon from Khartoum at that time.

After reviewing the most popular names, it is interesting, and perhaps surprising to see which names are absent. In none of the yearlong samples was there a boy named Paul, and only one Peter (in 1780). Likewise, there were no Michaels, Martins or Stephens – and, given Oswestry's links to the Northumbrian king, not a single Oswald!

Was it chance that the four sample years, 1580, 1680, 1780 and 1880, were unusual in being devoid of Oswalds? Might a more broadly-based survey have found that the name Oswald was indeed a popular choice in Oswestry and district through the generations, reflecting St Oswald's prominence in local life: in the dedication of the parish church, the stories associated with King Oswald's well, and the choice of St Oswald's feast day, August 5th, for one of Oswestry's annual fairs? You might well think so, but you would be wrong. Checking hundreds of local deeds and documents from mediaeval times to the 16th century failed to locate a single Oswald, and our church registers with just one exception have no examples of baby boys baptised with the name Oswald right through to early Victorian times. The exception, from May 1709, is an interesting one, and shows the parish officials giving the name Oswald to a foundling, "a child found in Mr John Price's porch in Church Street the 27th baptised the 28th".

The first example of parents choosing the name Oswald, from St Oswald's registers, dates back only to April 1844, when the infant Oswald Peploe Tudor, son of John Tudor, a naval commander, and his wife Margaret, of Upper Brook Street, was baptised. However, this was not the earliest example from Oswestry generally, as in September 1838, at Christ Church, Robert Oswald Davies had been baptised – he was the son of John Davies of Church Street, a draper, and his wife Ann. Slowly the name Oswald grew in popularity through the 19th century, with just one example from local baptism records in the 1840s, two in the 1850s, five in the 1860s, a fall back to just three in the 1870s, and then eight in both the 1880s and 1890s. In Shropshire generally, analysis of Shropshire registers using the online resource *Find My Past* identified ninety five Oswalds in total – except for our foundling, none were earlier than 1834, and around half of the total came from Oswestry and district.

Why did use of the name Oswald emerge in Oswestry at this time? In the first half of Victoria's reign it would not have been prompted by the church dedication as, at that time, the church was known simply as 'the parish church', or sometimes as St Mary's. However, the publication of Price's *History of Oswestry* (1815), William Cathrall's *History* (1855), and the writings of Askew Roberts in the *Advertizer* and elsewhere, led to an increasingly widespread awareness of the story of king Oswald and his links to Oswestry, and this is, I believe, the reason. The early examples, from the 1840s to the 1860s, come from Oswestry's middle classes – for the sons of a naval officer, a draper, an auctioneer, a watchmaker, and a master saddler, men who may have had the literacy skills, the means and the time, to acquire this knowledge. Other similar examples show families who had moved to Oswestry at this time, such as David Rees who moved here to manage the local branch of the North & South Wales Bank, marking their arrival here by naming their next child Oswald.

Finally, it is clear that the adoption of the name was encouraged by the trend for children to be given two Christian names rather than one. From 1875 to 1900, there were seventeen Oswalds baptised at St Oswald's and another five at Holy Trinity – of those twenty two, fully seventeen were given Oswald as their *middle* name. It was perhaps a way for parents to acknowledge or celebrate their links with Oswestry and with St Oswald, whilst still being able to choose a family name or a more popular name as their son's 'first' name.

*Based on articles printed in St Oswald's Parish Magazine for February 2017 and January 2018*

## Chapter 17: A study of local field names

Historians of Shropshire are very fortunate to have at their disposal a set of around five hundred hand drawn maps of the county, parish by parish, township by township. Prepared by George Foxall, these show in minute detail the field boundaries and field names taken from the tithe apportionment schedules and maps of 1836-50. As Mr Foxall said in his *Shropshire field names* (1980), the study of field names can tell us a great deal about our past – about land ownership, land use, soil quality, and agricultural practice, and about many other aspects of our local history. That said, compared to place names, or street names, written records of our field names are scarce, and the names themselves more ephemeral, more subject to change: as Mr Foxall said, "they tend to change from generation to generation, or as farm tenancies change, or even with the rotation of crops".

In this context, students of Oswestry's local history are lucky to have a set of surveys, from 1761, c.1790, and 1816, each predating the tithe apportionment, each survey giving the ownership, acreage and the names of fields within the liberties of the town and in the rural townships. Two of these surveys were made for the earl of Powis: the 1761 survey, made by Isaac Messeder, and limited to lands still belonging to the estate, is preserved at Powis Castle, with a photocopy available at the National Library of Wales; that of 1816 forms part of the National Library's holdings[45]. The third survey, of c.1790, including a set of detailed maps, township by township, prepared by Arthur Davies, forms part of the Oswestry Town Council archive[46].

---

45 NLW, Field book and plans of the Oswestry estate situate at and near the Town of Oswestry etc. belonging to the Right Honorable Henry Arthur, earl of Powis, 1761 (photocopy); M25, A survey and particular of estates in the parishes of Oswestry, Llanyblodwel, Llansilin, Llanymynech, St Martins and Ellesmere, etc. belonging to the Viscount Clive, 1816
46 OTC, A95, A survey of the several Townships & tythings within the Parish of Oswestry

Research on the lord's demesne estates in Oswestry, and in particular on the lord's two parks provides a suitable focus for studying these names. The lord's upper park, or *parc ucha*, lay to the west of the town on land that rises up towards Cyrn y Bwch (the Racecourse Common); whilst the smaller lower park, or *parc issa*, was situated to the south-east of the town, largely between Middleton Road and the lower part of Salop Road, including what is now College Road, the North Shropshire College campus, and the leisure centre. These two demesne parks have also been described, in less detail, in earlier surviving surveys and rentals of 1577, 1602, and 1607[47] but the present study has focussed largely on the field names and acreages contained in the three surveys from 1761 onwards, and in the tithe apportionment. This research has shown just how right Mr Foxall was to offer caution, and to stress how field names are subject to change. Also, whilst change in the naming of fields is common to the county as a whole, it is the case that, in Oswestry and other border areas, field names have also been subject to linguistic change – from English to Welsh, and vice versa – and from the vagaries caused when Welsh field names were written down by surveyors unaccustomed to the Welsh language.

By Tudor times, most field names in the Oswestry area were Welsh. In the town, there is some evidence of names becoming 'cymricised' from previous English names – for example, from *caldewellmor* to *goldwell croft* to *Ffynnon goulden* – but it is very likely that most of the fields in the upper park, and some at least of the fields in the lower park had Welsh names throughout their existence. In the lower park, the 1602 survey mentions five fields by name – '*Parke y Fynnon* or the Well Parke', '*Park y Llydiard* or the gate close', *gwerglodd y bechan*, *gwerglodd deito*, and the Park Lodge. The latter is a particularly interesting example of how names change over the years. In 1602, the surveyor John Norden noted as an aside that within the field there was "a little hill whereon the lodge is sayde sometyme to stand"– possibly it had formerly been a hunting lodge. The 1761 survey includes the field names *Lodger Onnen* and *Lodger Ithen* which, if seen entirely on their own, would present a puzzle; the 1816 survey gives clearer spellings, *Lodge yr onnen* and *Lodge yr eithen*, signifying the presence of ash trees and broom respectively. However, in Mr Foxall's map, based on the 1838 tithe apportionment, the former has become Barton's Field, the latter Perkins Lodge – and in neither case can the apparent surname be linked to the landowner or the tenant of the day.

---

47   W.J. Slack, *Lordship of Oswestry, 1393-1607* (1951), p56-57

Turning to the 400-acre upper park, a comparison of the patterns of fields described in the four surveys from 1761 to 1838 reveals a complex picture. In the westernmost fields, and also the fields closest to the town, this analysis reveals a gradual change from smaller fields to larger ones. In the area between, the reverse has occurred: many of the fields have been subdivided, probably as a result of small-scale industrial activity, reflected in field names such as Brick Kiln Meadow and Coalpit Field. Sizeable areas of woodland shown on the earlier surveys have disappeared by the time of the tithe maps, as have field names in the upper park such as *Cae Coediog* ('wooded field'). One other name to have fallen from use in the years leading up the tithe apportionment was *Cae Stanny*, a field name which seems to hark back to the Stanneys, a prominent family in civic and commercial life in Oswestry and district from the late 15th century through to the late 17th century. The 1761 survey noted two adjacent fields, taken together, around 25 acres in size, both with this name. The name survived to the c.1790 and 1816 surveys but not to the tithe map, which shows instead six smaller fields, with the names Middle Field, Upper Field, Little Wheat Field, Big Lowsy Meadow, and Plantation, and the less prosaic *Pwll y Flownog* (probably *pwll y fawnog*, the word *mawnog* signifying a peat-bog).

In places such as Oswestry, as elsewhere along the Welsh border, the process of change from Welsh to English often occurred (where it did at all) in comparatively recent times. Some of the English field names shown in Mr Foxall's maps of Oswestry and district may have been only of every recent usage. Field names in the upper park such as Banky Field, Thorn Field, Thistly Field and the Meadow, may tell us something of those fields from the perspective of the farm worker of the 1830s, but they are 'new' names, replacing names like *Cae Mawr, Cae Berllan, Cae Itha* and *Cae Nessa*[48]. Meanwhile, two apparently Welsh names that are included on the tithe map, in the far south-western corner of the park, *Cae Withy Tyn* and *Cae Buck*, serve only to confuse us by encouraging thought of withy beds and deer – when, in reality, the names can be tracked back to the former *cae wrth y ty* (simply, 'field by the house') and *cae bach* ('small field').

---

48  These names signify Big Field, Orchard Field, Lower Field and Nearer Field

Not everywhere will be as fortunate as Oswestry, with its four major surveys from 1761 to 1838, but most parishes will have a number of deeds and documents, recording transfers of ownership of land and property, from mediaeval times and later. Whilst these may not provide a comprehensive picture, providing details for only a small number of fields, nevertheless, once stitched together with other information, it may nevertheless be possible to sketch out the pattern of fields, and their names, over many years, and perhaps from Tudor times. Research on the background to the 17th century historian John Davies of Middleton highlighted the number of deeds relating to land in Middleton that survive in the collections at Shrewsbury and the National Library[49]. These earlier documents cast clear light on a field name shown on the Middleton tithe map, the unusual name *Godferydd*. In this case, an earlier estate survey, of 1763, had failed to help, giving the equally puzzling *Gadfar Hays*, but documents from 1547-51 and 1675 provided the names *Goedva Here* and *Goedfa Hir*, explaining the field name as 'the long wood'.

The lower park and upper park belonged to the lord and remained part of the manorial estate through to modern times. As a result, for the fields in those two parks, we cannot expect to find other deeds and documents to supplement the information that we have gleaned from estate surveys. However, this is not the case with other parts of the lord's demesne as these lands had been sold off in 1570 as fee farms by the earl of Arundel, Henry FitzAlan. The lands sold included a number of fields (including Glovers Meadow and the Rod Meadows) just south of the lower park, and a hundred acres of land known as the 'over hayes' immediately below the upper park. Records surviving at the John Rylands Library in Manchester[50] provide a detailed description of the Over Hayes (in later years known simply as the Hayes) in 1570, including the field names *cae kodoge, cae eskob, croked close, kai'r ffynnon, foxeburye close, bromley close*, and *longe meadowe*. Only three of these names survived to the surveys of c.1790 and 1816, where they are listed as *Cae Coediog*[51], Foxberry and Well Field, and only one (Well Field) lasted to the tithe apportionment. On the tithe map, Foxberry had been replaced by Gravel Hole Piece, whilst *Cae Coediog* had changed to yet another Banky Field.

---

49  See *Trans. Shrops. Arch. & Hist. Soc.*, 75 (2000), 85-86
50  University of Manchester, John Rylands Library, Latin 274, f.370b
51  This is a different *Cae Coediog* to the field of the same name in the upper park

It is an ever-changing picture, with changes to names, to spelling and pronunciation, and, particularly in border areas such as ours, changes in language. Fields can 'disappear', being merged to form larger units; fields can be split up; and they can expand or contract, as boundary markers are moved. More so than with place names, river names or street names, field names can present us with a challenge, being hard to tie down, and difficult to map out. This being so, Mr Foxall's work, undertaken over many years, is an immense achievement, valuable both as a stand-alone 'snapshot' of the county in about 1840, and as a solid foundation or starting point for historians seeking to reconstruct field patterns from previous centuries.

*Originally printed in the Salopian Recorder, the newsletter of the Friends of Shropshire Archives, for Summer 2010*

## Chapter 18: Welsh surnames in Oswestry and district

In former times, most children born in Wales took on the name of their father, being described as son of (*ap*, or *ab*) or daughter of (*ferch*) – for example Edward ap Robert, or Elizabeth ferch Richard – rather than having permanent surnames such as Roberts, Butcher or Weston that were passed down from generation to generation. Studies of the subject have been greatly strengthened by the publication of *Welsh surnames* by Professor T.J. Morgan and Dr Prys Morgan. This is both a study of the development of surnames in Wales and the Welsh border, and a dictionary of those names with, in each case, many examples of those names from old deeds and documents. One of the many sources used by the authors was Oswestry's parish registers; numerous examples of names are cited from our local registers, which survive from 1558.

It is well known that, in Oswestry, the use of *ap* and *ferch* in names was very common, from mediaeval times through to the early 18th century. This was the case both in the town and especially in the surrounding countryside. For example, a deed of 1533 recorded the sale of a house in Church Street by Maurice ap Thomas ap Richard to David ap Sir Richard and his wife Katherine verch John. The house stood next to a barn owned by Meredith ap Guttyn. The transaction was witnessed by the lord's steward, Richard Herbert, the two bailiffs John ap David ap Rees and Edward Meredith, and by Ieuan ap Llywelyn, Nicholas ap Thomas, Maurice ap Guttyn and Edward Saer. Just to prove Oswestry's Welsh credentials, 'saer' is Welsh for carpenter.

This form of naming was the case with the indigenous population, and to a great extent with families that had moved into the town from surrounding English counties, such as the Stanneys from Cheshire and the Mucklestons from the Shropshire/Staffordshire borders. The parish registers for the late 16th century include hybrid names such as Edward ap Thomas Stanney and Katherine verch Richard ap Rondle Muckleston, both of whom died in 1587, and Augustine ap Philip Langford, who was baptised at St Oswald's in 1591. The latter is an interesting case: you would have expected the son of Philip Langford to be another Langford, but records from the shoemakers' guild and the parish registers show that in his adult life he abandoned his father's surname to become Augustine Phillips. Quite a challenge for a family historian!

There is no firm evidence that St Oswald's ever had a vicar with an 'ap' name, though it is possible, but by no means certain, that a man who we know only by his Christian name Matthew, vicar of Oswestry in the 1520s, was a Matthew ap David, and that Richard Hova, vicar in 1416 began life as Richard ap Hwfa. John Price, vicar from the mid-sixteenth century until his death in 1583, was the son of John ap Thomas ap Rees, the vicar's name showing the change from 'ap Rees' to 'Price'. Also, from 1521 to 1552, possibly later, St Oswald's was served by a curate Owen ap David. Likewise, the churchwardens included numerous examples, particularly from the rural townships. For instance, in 1599 the four wardens included Thomas ap David ap Nicholas and Richard ap John ap Meredith of Pentregaer, and in 1610 they included Richard ap Hugh of Sweeney and Hugh ap Kadwaladr, a leading Oswestry glover.

There was a gradual decline in the number and proportion of children baptised in Oswestry with *ap* and *ferch* names, through the 17th century with the practice continuing in Oswestry and district through into the second decade of the 18th century, eventually being overtaken by anglicised forms such as Jones, Davies, Edwards, Williams and Roberts.

*Largely based on an article printed in St Oswald's Parish Magazine for November 2009.*

## Chapter 19: Catering for Welsh speakers

The historic parish of St Oswald's, from mediaeval times through to the 1820s and 1830s, was very large, stretching from the townships of Pentregaer and Cynynion on the Welsh border across to Middleton, Aston and Wootton, and south to Crickheath. For much of this time, many parishioners, in both the town and the surrounding countryside, would have been Welsh speaking. Many local place names, field names and personal names all testify to this fact. Our early churchwardens' accounts, for the years 1579 to 1615, show that the church was catering for both English and Welsh speaking parishioners. The accounts for 1584/85 record the payment of seven pence "for the bindinge of the welsh Psalter"; in 1588/89, there was a payment of eleven shillings for part payment "for the welsh bible and Salter"; in 1598/99, the churchwarden John Williams paid three shillings and eight pence for a Welsh book of common prayer and sixpence for two Welsh catechisms. Finally, in 1611/12, the wardens paid five shillings for a Welsh communion book.

Other records show how the church sought always to ensure that there were clergy who were Welsh speaking, normally with one or more Welsh speaking curates available to support the vicar. This was the case from pre-Reformation times, when the clergy were appointed by Shrewsbury Abbey, through to the early 19th century. Largely forgotten by history, records from property deeds and from wills show that the clerk Owen ap David served St Oswald's as curate from at least 1521 to 1552, and so would have witnessed wholesale change in the life of the church over this thirty year period. Another Welsh curate was John Davies, who served from 1592 to 1624; the burial of his widow Lowri is recorded in February 1625. The famous Welsh poet Goronwy Owen was a curate here in the 1740s.

Visitors to Oswestry in 1801 noted that there were large painted boards, in the "cross aisle", setting out the Ten Commandments, the Lord's Prayer, and the Creed, all in Welsh, something that the travellers had not seen in any of the churches that they had visited in Wales[52]. Welsh services ceased at St Oswald's in 1814, transferring to a room over the Town Clerk's office on the Bailey Head at this time. It seems that these services ceased with the establishment of new churches at Trefonen in 1821 and at Rhydycroesau in 1838, which sought to cater for the needs of the Welsh speaking parts of the parish. However, the establishment in Oswestry of a number of Welsh speaking chapels – Calvinistic Methodists in Castle Street and then in Gatacre Place (Seion) from 1813; Congregationalists on the Bailey Head and then Chapel Street (Hermon) from 1840; Wesleyan Methodists also from around 1840, from 1857 in Penylan Lane and from 1878 in Victoria Road (Horeb); and Baptists from around 1860 in Willow Street, then the Rope Walk and Castle Street (Penuel) – brought into sharp relief the fact that there was no Church of England provision for Welsh speakers within the town.

No action was taken, on this important issue as with others, during the long incumbency of the Rev. Thomas Salwey. He resigned in January 1871, and it was not long before this gap in provision was addressed, with the bishop of St Asaph, Joshua Hughes, at the heart of developments. A Welsh speaker himself, the bishop is described in *Welsh biography online* as "a great Welsh preacher" and as "a great patriot, passionately devoted to Wales, her language, her people, and her spiritual well-being" who "preached in Welsh at every opportunity and insisted on an adequate provision of Welsh services". When the Rev. Canon W. Howell Evans' name was put forward as the next vicar of St Oswald's, the successor to the Rev. Thomas Salwey, the bishop was concerned that he was not a Welsh speaker, and that, at the time, St Oswald's had no Welsh speaking curates. The bishop's objection to the appointment was only withdrawn when an undertaking was given that a Welsh speaking curate would be appointed.

---

52   NLW, 1340C; see also J. Pryce-Jones, *An Oswestry miscellany* (2007), p23-27

The Rev. Howell Evans commenced his ministry in Oswestry in February 1872, and in July 1872 services in Welsh began on the lower floor of the Victoria Rooms.  From the start, numbers were encouraging, proving the need for services in Welsh: five years later, the *Advertizer* commented that "the Welsh congregation increased under the earnest ministrations of the late curate, the Rev. William Williams, now vicar of Llanuwchllyn [and later Dean of St David's], and of the present curate, the Rev. D. Evans", sufficient that plans were drawn up to build a Welsh church.  Fund raising took place, the chief subscribers being the earl of Powis, Sir Watkin Williams Wynn, the bishop of St Asaph and the vicar, and on Tuesday June 26$^{th}$ 1877 the new church, an "iron structure" of the type known colloquially as 'tin tabernacles', was opened, in what was then known as the new churchyard, in Welsh Walls.

The church cost £470 to build, and comprised a nave and apse, with vestry and organ chamber, and open deal seating for 270 people.  The *Advertizer* commented that "while we cannot share the opinion that the new church is an ornament to the churchyard in which it stands, we are ready to admit that it has as comely an appearance as it seems possible for an iron structure to have".  Mrs Howell of Tenby, also the donor of the pulpit in the parish church, provided three stained glass windows, including a central window depicting the crucifixion; the windows being supplied by Messrs Jones & Willis of Birmingham.

The first service to be held in the new church began, in St Oswald's, at 11 o'clock, before the congregation, led by the choir, processed to St David's. singing 'Onward Christian Soldiers' in Welsh.  The sermon was preached by the bishop of St Asaph, who took his text from 2 Corinthians, chapter 4, verse 7.  Other parts of the service were led by the curate, the Rev. David Evans, the Rev. D. Davies of Llansilin, the Rev. D.P. Evans of Trefonen, the Rev. J.D. Jones of Colwyn, and the Rev. W. Williams of Llanuwchllyn.  Other clergy present included the vicar, and the rector of Rhydycroesau, the Rev. Canon Williams.

The iron church remained in use for thirty five years, before plans were made for its replacement by a more permanent brick, stone and concrete building, designed by local architect W.H. Spaull, and built by local building contractor William Felton.  Architect, builder and also the vicar, the Rev. W.M.B. Lutener, were Freemasons, and the foundation stone for the new church was laid on July 24$^{th}$ 1912, with elaborate Masonic ceremony, by the Grand Master for the Province of Shropshire, Sir Offley Wakeman, with Freemasons from all over Shropshire and beyond, present.  There had been a procession from Lower Brook Street to St Oswald's, for a special service.  The *Advertizer* described how "the panoply of robe and collar and chain glittered handsomely in the prevailing sunlight, while in the church itself the electric light which sought to illumine the scene glinted upon gold and medals and jewels with impressive effect". From the parish church, the procession moved on to the site of the new church, for the ceremonial laying of the foundation stone by the Grand Master, after he had first given a lengthy address. The foundation stone, inscribed in Welsh, was set in place with a "handsome ivory handled silver trowel, suitably inscribed, supplied by Brother Lashmore", the local silversmith.

Less than 10 months later, the new church was opened, being ceremonially unlocked by the Venerable Archdeacon D.R. Thomas, following a service in St Oswald's, and a procession, preceded by cross and banners, to the new church. In contrast to the foundation stone laying ceremony, this time the services and the processions were "of the simplest character".

Mr Spaull's building was described as being of "the Early English period of Gothic architecture"; "all ornament has been eschewed on the score of economy" but nevertheless "the church presents a pleasing appearance internally and externally", noted the *Advertizer*. The red brick, and terracotta window dressings, were from Ruabon; the chancel arch was of Corsham Down stone. The three stained glass windows from the iron church were incorporated in the new building. Interestingly, the *Advertizer* reported that there had been "some difficulty as to the foundations" given the building's location in the former churchyard. Problems had been "overcome by excavating between the graves to the solid undisturbed earth, piling the excavations with concrete and putting in a bed of re-inforced concrete from one pier to the next, on which the walls were built".

St David's remained in use until falling numbers led to its closure as a church in August 1985[53]. Subsequently it was used for a number of years by the Oswestry & District Amateur Operatic Society before, in 2014, it was acquired for conversion to residential use.

*Based on articles printed in St Oswald's Parish Magazine for July and August 2014, subsequently reprinted in the Oswestry Advertizer in February 2016*

---

53  The author is grateful for information provided by Anne Pilsbury

# Chapter 20: A grand musical festival

It is known that Oswestry's parish church acquired a new church organ in 1812, built by William Allen of London, and paid for by public subscription. The instrument was installed in a new gallery constructed across the chancel arch and cutting off the view of the altar from the bulk of the congregation.

The installation of the new organ was marked by "a grand musical festival". Askew Roberts, writing in 1880[54], noted that "there are those living yet who attended it", adding that "one lady who did has kept a programme of the second day's performances. The tickets of admission were a Guinea each, and the performers came from London. The Messiah was given the first day, and Selections on the second. Mrs Salmon sang 'With Verdure Clad' [from Haydn's 'Creation'] and Mr Bradbury 'Deeper and Deeper Still' [from Handel's 'Jephta']. There was a full orchestra, and a London conductor. All the fashionables of the district attended, including the 'Ladies of Llangollen'".

It would be interesting to know if the copy of the concert programme that Mr Roberts had seen, or indeed any other copies, may have survived to the present day. Nevertheless, the Vestry Minute Books provide us with an insight into the event. The minutes for September 2$^{nd}$ 1812 record how William Price, a local bookseller, printer and the publisher of the well known *History of Oswestry* (1815), had received a letter from Mr Charles Jane Ashley "offering to open the organ with oratorios to be performed on the 24$^{th}$ and 25$^{th}$ instant and proposing that the surplus arising from the receipts of the money taken at the church doors and theatre after defraying the Expence of the performers shall be divided into two equal parts the one of which shall be taken by Mr Ashley and the other appropriated for the benefit of the Church Charity Schools in the town". Mr Price brought the letter to the Vestry for its consideration, and the meeting agreed that the vicar, the Rev. J.W. Bourke, should write back to Mr Ashley to accept his offer, though, as prudent custodians of the parish, the members resolved that "It is to be distinctly understood that the Committee does not make itself accountable for any expences which might be incurred in providing for the oratorios and concert or in the performers' engagements or otherwise but that the whole responsibility is to be undertaken by Mr Ashley".

---

54 'Oswestry ecclesiastical history: the old church', *Trans. Shrops. Arch. Soc.*, 3 (1880), 185-186

Mr Ashley (1772-1843) was a cellist, who played at Ranelagh Gardens in Chelsea and at Covent Garden. He was the son of John Ashley, a bassoonist and conductor, and was part of a remarkable musical family who organised concerts and musical festivals across the country for more than fifty years including the first performances in England of the 'Creation' and of Mozart's 'Requiem', bringing choral music to a much wider audience than hitherto. The soloist Eliza Salmon (1787-1849), a soprano, had taken part in the first Covent Garden performance of the 'Messiah' in 1805; she was "gifted with a voice of beautiful tone, a charming manner and a face 'of dazzling fairness'". It is clear to see why the two-day festival was remembered, many years on: it must have been a major event in Oswestry's social calendar of the time.

The Allen organ was described as being "of an exceedingly rich and sweet tone". It was added to in 1858, these improvements being made by Messrs Gray & Davidson, and was then superseded by the Hill organ at the time of the restoration of the church in 1872/74.

*Based on an article printed in St Oswald's Parish Magazine for January 2009*

# Chapter 21: Roberts the Gas

One of the paintings and portraits adorning the walls of the Guildhall depicts a cheery Victorian gentleman, posing with a copy of the *Illustrated London News* and a clay pipe laid out on the table beside him, and with a full glass of wine or port in his hand. The subject of the painting is Robert Roberts, the man who brought gas lighting to Oswestry. The portrait in former times used to hang on the wall of the smoking room of Osburn's Hotel in Bailey Street[55].

Gas lighting, derived from coal, was first developed by the Scottish engineer William Murdoch. Working for the well known firm of Boulton & Watt, Murdoch carried out experiments with flammable gases seeking to establish which gas worked best for illuminating lamps. In 1792, he managed to light his home in Cornwall with gas, and in 1798 he illuminated the main building of Messrs Boulton & Watt's Soho Works, in Birmingham, using gas. Initially seen as a means of lighting factories and works, gas lighting was soon recognised as a means of lighting streets, and private houses; Pall Mall in central London was lit by gas in 1807.

Mr Roberts moved to Oswestry from Merionethshire at the very start of the 19th century, establishing a successful plumbing and glazing business. He lived in the half-timbered house at the junction of Lower Brook Street and Upper Church Street, next to his workshops. Building on his plumbing skills, he expanded into gas, developing Oswestry's first gas works at premises in Willow Street on the edge of the town.

Next door to his works was the New Theatre (later a malthouse), built by Colonel Ormsby Gore, and the theatre became the first public building in Oswestry to be lit by gas. William Cathrall's *History of Oswestry* (1855) tells us that "Mr Charles Stanton, at that time Manager of the Oswestry Theatre, which had been recently built, entered into an arrangement with Mr Roberts to light the Theatre during the season. Mr Roberts had been hitherto experimenting on a small scale, and was not fully prepared to enter upon so important a piece of work as illuminating the Theatre. His persevering habits prevailed, and he agreed with Mr Stanton that the Theatre should be lighted on a certain evening. To introduce gas into a large public building was deemed an event of no common magnitude in those days. The appointed evening, in September 1819, at length arrived, and Mr Roberts succeeded in lighting the Theatre with a brilliant gas, which astonished all beholders. The performances on that evening were for the benefit of Miss Stanton, the Manager's daughter".

The illumination of Willow Street soon followed, and by 1821 the short-lived *Oswestry Herald* was reporting enthusiastically that "from the praiseworthy example set by the inhabitants of Willow Street we shall soon have the pleasure of seeing the whole of the town illuminated this winter with gas". Shortly later, the inhabitants of Bailey Street joined together, subscribing with Mr Roberts for street lights to be installed and supplied with gas. Mr Cathrall described how "places of religious worship soon afterwards adopted gas. The Welsh Methodist Chapel, in Willow Street, first used it; the Wesleyan Methodist Chapel, Salop Road, followed; and the Old Parish Church ... was afterwards lighted, forty burners being introduced, including lights at the entrance doors". Mr Roberts first proposed to light St Oswald's with gas in 1824 but it is not immediately clear whether gas lighting was installed at that stage. In 1831 though it is clear that the church was giving the matter serious consideration as Mr Roberts was "held bound to furnish gas without any offensive smell"; such a smell could not "be permitted upon any terms, and if the officiating minister [should] complain at any time that the gas is offensive, Mr Roberts [should] not be paid anything for that night".

Thomas Owen, writing in 1904, described a list, from 1854, which showed that the cost of illuminating the church with gas light for the year amounted to £16 and four shillings, paid by individual subscription; he commented that "the sums subscribed [for the year, by members of the congregation] ranged from a shilling to a pound, many of the 'big' people of that time having 'little' figures appended to their names". Mr Owen also recalled an incident one Autumn Sunday evening when, with the money not forthcoming, the churchwardens ordered that the lights remain off, so that "by the time the preacher ascended the pulpit, he could hardly see to read his text". Mr Owen continued; "Well, the preacher stood up, grim and stern, and administered such a rebuke to the congregation for their petty parsimony that they never forgot. On the following Sunday, the proper lighting was resumed"[56].

The other places of religious worship quickly followed the example; and in a very few years gas became the universal light in all public places, private houses, and commercial and trading establishments.

---

56  T. Owen, *Personal reminiscences of Oswestry fifty years ago*, 85

Robert Roberts, gas proprietor.
Reproduced here with permission of Oswestry Town Council.

The installation of gas lighting was not a straight forward business. Pipes needed to be installed to supply the gas to the premises, or to the street concerned, and to make branches off the main pipe to each property which took out a contract with Mr Roberts. An advertisement dated October 4th 1821 set out the charges for one, two or three single jets, or for various combinations where a number of jets were set on a single bracket, and with charges based upon use for an agreed number of hours. Under the contract terms Mr Roberts would install pipework only to "just within the house, and to supply the light when the interior is fitted up and made air tight which must be done by each individual". The householder also had to ensure that a glass was fitted over each burner "as three or four times the quantity of Gas is consumed, accompanied with an extremely offensive odour, when this rule is departed from". "The Proprietor recommends the use of the Straight Chimney Glasses, in which the Gas burns with a much steadier light than in any others". All this interior work was the responsibility of the householder but this work had to be carried out by Mr Roberts "and paid for on completion of the work".

That said, the lighting would not have been brilliant as for most of the 19th century, gas lights were simply naked flames. Whilst these were much brighter than candles or oil lamps, they were poor by modern standards. Things improved after 1885, with the invention of the modern gas mantle. St Oswald's remained gas lit until the first decade of the 20th century when electricity was introduced.

Mr Roberts' enterprise prospered. In 1842, he moved his gas works from Willow Street to larger premises at the foot of Victoria Road, the new works comprising "a retort house, purifying house, with a large tank and gasometer. The apparatus is of the usual character, including condenser, purifier, scrub, with fire clay retorts, hydraulic main, &c. The chimney is square, and spiral in form, tapering to the top". For many years the gas works and gas holders were a prominent sight, located between the cemetery and the old football ground, greeting visitors approaching the town from Shrewsbury over the railway bridge, still known today as the gasworks bridge.

In 1855, Cathrall could note that "the lighting of the borough ... is still under the superintendence of Mr Roberts, who, now an octogenarian, is of hale health, and of as active and bustling habits as he was in the days of his youth". In fact Mr Roberts only relinquished control of the business in 1860, when the Oswestry Gas Light and Coke Company was incorporated; Mr Roberts holding a tenth of the one thousand shares, with other major shareholdings held by the banker James Thomas Jones of Brynhafod, David Lloyd of the Wynnstay Arms, the railway contractor Thomas Savin and the solicitor Joseph Bassett. This company continued to provide gas to the town until 1948 when the gas industry was nationalised.

Described by Isaac Watkin as "a man of much talent and of singular industry", and by Thomas Owen as "a short, fussy little man, and though slightly lame, [one who] moved about with the aid of his inseparable stick, with the quickness of a pea on a vibrating drum-head", Robert Roberts died on December 15th 1861, aged 85. The *Advertizer* reported that its "list of deaths this week contains the name of one who for many years has been one of the oldest tradesmen in the town. We allude to Mr Roberts the late gas proprietor. He has been in business in the town for between fifty and sixty years – for forty two of which he was connected with the gas works of the town. We believe Mr Roberts first introduced gas into the county of Salop"[57].

The funeral service took place on December 19th at St Oswald's and was conducted by the curate the Rev. George Cuthbert, followed by burial in the churchyard. His remains were interred next to those of his first wife Elizabeth, who had died in 1835, their infant daughter Mary who had died in 1801 aged two years and four months, and Robert's niece Ellen (d.1860) who had lived at their Brook Street home as a member of the family for twenty years or more. Also buried in the grave plot was his infant son Robert, who died in 1840 aged two years and six months, Mr Roberts having re-married in November 1836. His second wife, Mary, had formerly been married to a local surgeon John Edwards (d. 1831); she died in 1867 and was buried with her first husband[58].

*Based on an article printed in St Oswald's Parish Magazine for December 2012*

---

57 *Personal reminiscences*, 20; Oswestry Advertizer, 18 December 1861. The notice recorded his death at his residence in Brook Street
58 See J.A. Roberts, 'Oswestry old church monuments', *Trans. Shrops. Arch. Soc.*, 6 (1883), 161-162, 176

## Chapter 22: History reflected in stained glass

Many visitors to St Oswald's comment upon its many impressive stained glass windows, something which is reflected in the 2006 edition of Sir Nikolaus Pevsner's architectural guide to Shropshire. With the exception of the millennium window behind the font, all the stained glass in the church was installed between 1861 and 1892, the makers including David Evans of Shrewsbury, Messrs Clayton & Bell, James Ballantine & Son, Pilkington's, and Messrs Heaton, Butler & Bayne. The Pevsner's guide lists several of those windows, but does not mention the west window and, as it is natural to look towards the east end of the church, this window is perhaps less well known, more infrequently examined than our other windows, than perhaps it deserves to be.

The west window was one of several that were filled with stained glass in the immediate aftermath of G.E. Street's restorations of 1872/74. Street's work had included the renewal of the window tracery in each of the nave windows, and the installation of the present window in the east end of the Lady Chapel, where there had previously been a doorway. The list of subscriptions towards the cost of this work included sums totalling £1,000 for six new stained glass windows which were then installed in the three years after the church re-opened in 1874 replacing plain glass which had been fitted ready for the re-opening.

The subscribers list indicates that one of the new windows was to be funded by "the Misses Croxon" of the Lawn, the imposing red brick house facing the present Park Gates. At that time, the Lawn was a substantial family home, with large and impressive gardens. A map, dated June 1883, when the property was offered for sale, shows that the gardens extended all the way back to Roft Street, encompassing the present commercial properties in Smithfield Street including Denny's garage, as well as Marks & Spencer in Smithfield Road and the public car park behind it.

Moving to Oswestry in the mid-18th century when John Croxon of Wrexham married the daughter and heiress of Richard Jones, a Cross Street butcher, the Croxons became key figures in local life, remaining so for over a hundred years. John Croxon, like his father-in-law a butcher, was made a freeman of the borough in 1772, as was his infant son Richard. John was elected Mayor of Oswestry in 1778, as was Richard in 1801; another son, John, was Mayor in 1812. Richard's son, a third John, was Mayor in 1836; his younger brother Richard Jones Croxon was Town Clerk from 1832 to 1864. The Croxons built up a sizeable portfolio of land and property, including lands beyond Roft Street towards what is now Park Street; Ferrers Road was developed immediately after the sale of the Lawn, the name deriving from Henry Ferrers Croxon, grandson of the Mayor of 1812. Croxon's Square, on the bend of Roft Street, and now largely replaced by Regent Court, was built by the family towards the end of the 18th century. They also invested in coal mines in Trefarclawdd and Trefonen, and were founding partners in 1792 of the Oswestry Old Bank.

The Lawn, Church Street, a view of the rear of the house and its gardens. From *The gossiping guide to Wales* (1886).

The Misses Croxon, donors of our west window, were four unmarried daughters of Richard Croxon of the Lawn and his wife Frances. Frances (1796-1883), Alice (1802-1882), Elizabeth (1805-1878) and Sarah (1808-1873) were the sisters of the third John Croxon (d. 1869) and Richard Jones Croxon (d. 1875). In 1871, the Census lists Richard Jones Croxon, solicitor, living at the Lawn, with three of his sisters, and a number of domestic servants. The 1881 Census shows the then surviving sisters Frances and Alice living there, with their cousin and heir Henry Ferrers Croxon, 33, his family, and seven live-in servants.

Turning to the window, which was set up in memory of the sisters' parents Richard Croxon (d. 1838) and his wife Frances (d. 1857), the three central panels show Christ appearing to the disciples gathered in the upper room on the evening of Easter Day, with the text (Luke, 24:45) "Then opened he their understanding, that they might understand the scriptures". The left-hand panel shows Jesus' appearance to St Mary Magdalene outside the empty tomb, with the text: "I am not yet ascended" (John, 20:17). Finally, the right-hand panel illustrates the recommissioning of St Peter with the text "feed my lambs, feed my sheep" (John, 21:15-21).

The stained glass was fitted in 1877; it was one of seven windows whose stained glass was provided by the well known firm of Clayton & Bell of London.

*Based on an article printed in St Oswald's Parish Magazine for February 2014*

# Chapter 23: The builders of Plas Wilmot, Wilfred Owen's birthplace - their family background

Oswestry rightly is proud of its connection with Wilfred Owen, born at Plas Wilmot on March 18th 1893. His ancestry through the Salter family is well rooted in Oswestry's history. His parents were married at St Oswald's on December 8th 1891, the church registers recording the marriage of Tom Owen, 29, living at Underdale Road, Shrewsbury, a [railway] clerk, the son of William Owen, a commercial traveller, and Harriet Susan Shaw, 24, of Plas Wilmot, daughter of Edward Shaw, ironmonger. The witnesses included the bride's father and her sister Mrs Mary Salter Loughrey. The officiating minister was the Rev. Thomas Redfern, vicar of Holy Trinity. The wedding is likely to have been a very sombre one, as it was little more than a week since the death of the bride's mother Mary, and Susan wore black for the service. In the 1891 Census, Tom Owen, then aged 28, had been listed in Shrewsbury, living with his parents, and described as a railway accountant.

After the wedding the couple lived at Plas Wilmot with Susan's father. Tom and Susan Owen had four children – Wilfred and Mary born in Oswestry in 1893 and 1896 respectively, and then, after Edward Shaw's death in January 1897, and the sale of Plas Wilmot, William Harold (1897) was born in Shrewsbury, and Colin (1900) was born in Birkenhead. The family moved back to Shrewsbury in 1907.

Edward Shaw had moved to Oswestry from Herefordshire in 1850. He was a successful ironmonger with premises in Bailey Street, and later in Cross Street. He was a magistrate, a councillor, and Mayor of Oswestry in 1869. He was one of the four churchwardens at the time of the major rebuilding of St Oswald's in 1872/74.

Edward Shaw moved to Plas Wilmot as a result of his marriage in 1857 to Mary Salter, one of five children of Edward and Mary Salter, who had built Plas Wilmot in 1829/30. Mr Shaw's bride had inherited Plas Wilmot fifteen years earlier, on the death of her mother. Mr & Mrs Shaw made Plas Wilmot their home; they had four children – Mary Salter Shaw (1860), Emma Yeld Shaw (1861), Edward Gough Shaw (1863), and Harriet Susan Shaw (1867). Mary and Emma were baptised at St Oswald's, the younger two at Holy Trinity: Susan was baptised on April 15th 1867.

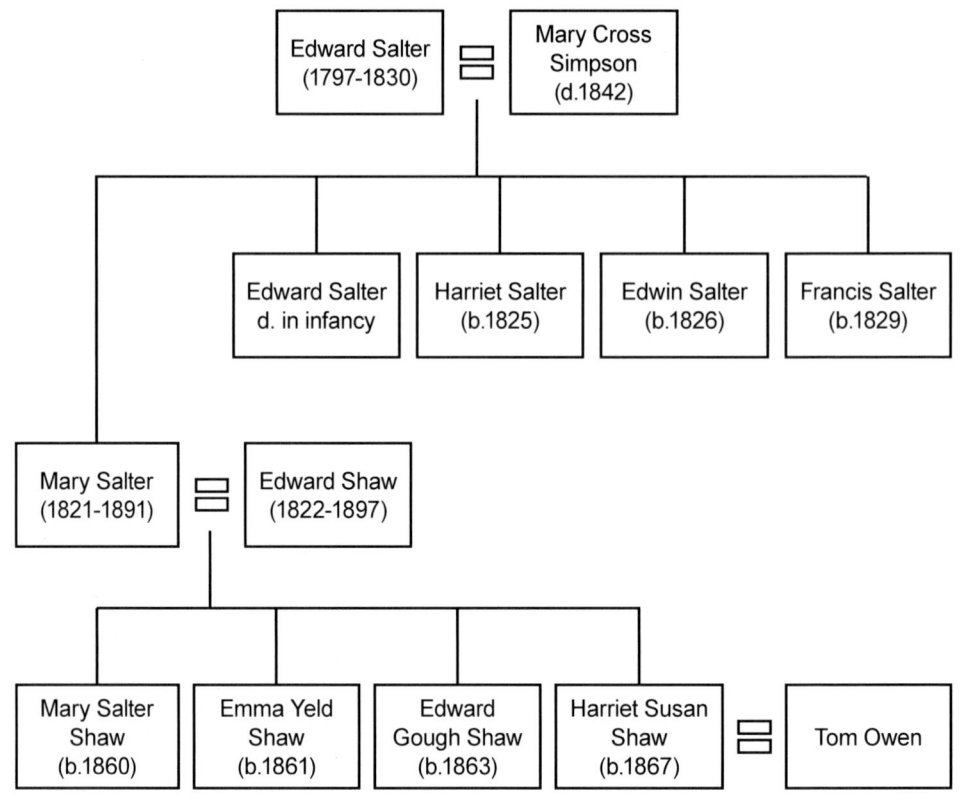

Wilfred Owen's ancestry: descendants of Edward Salter and Mary Cross Simpson.

Biographers of Wilfred Owen often mention the Salter family and their long links with Oswestry's history. Dominic Hibberd, in his *Wilfred Owen, a new biography* (2002), wrote that "There had been ... Salters in Oswestry since the 13th century or earlier, their name and wealth originating from the brine springs of Shropshire and Cheshire"[59] acknowledging that "establishing links beyond [the early 18th century] might be difficult".

---

59  Isaac Watkin (1920), describing the 18th and 19th century Salters, commented that "the Salters were a large family about the time of Henry III and their home appears to have been in Oswestry, though it is said they made their wealth by manufacturing salt from the brine springs of North Shropshire and Cheshire"

It is true that the names Salter and le Salter occur regularly in Oswestry's mediaeval history, in early surviving property deeds for Oswestry, such as a deed of the first half of the 13th century, witnessed by John le Salter, and two deeds of the second half of the 13th century, one recording the purchase of land called Bradley, modern day Bradley Fields, by Alice, widow of John le Salter, and the other detailing the purchase of property in *Wilesystrete*, modern day Willow Street, by Richard son of John le Salter. Government records show that in 1265 Alice le Salter of *Oswaldestre* took a complaint to Westminster against the Mayor and bailiffs of Winchester "that 28 sacks of wool which her men were taking to London from Winchester Fair had been arrested at Guildford"[60]. The two earliest surviving wills relating to Oswestry are those of Richard le Salter (1335) and of Richard son of Richard le Salter (1373); and records of those who served each year as bailiffs for the town – two bailiffs being elected each year until 1674 when the position was replaced by that of Mayor – show that on numerous occasions between 1315 and 1495 one of the bailiffs was a Salter[61].

However, the name Salter then drops out of local records, with only sporadic instances from 1500 onwards. There are no further Salter bailiffs prior to the abolition of that role in 1673 and there were no Salter mayors in the years between the creation of the post of mayor of Oswestry in 1673/74 and the changes to the Oswestry Corporation brought about in 1835. Also, examination of Oswestry's parish registers indicates only seven Salter entries between 1558 and 1603, and then none at all between 1603 and 1760. It seems unlikely therefore that there was a direct link between the mediaeval Salters and the more modern Salters from whom Wilfred Owen was descended.

Indeed, we can be confident in pinpointing the date of the family's arrival in Oswestry, as apprenticeship records show that in 1743 Joseph Salter was apprenticed to John Gardiner, an Oswestry clockmaker. Joseph was the son of Richard Salter of Little Ness and his wife Ann. Richard and Ann had married in 1725 at Meole Brace; he was described as of the parish of Baschurch, she of Shrawardine. Joseph was born in December 1726, and baptised at Little Ness. A daughter Elizabeth was born a year later. It is probable that there was another son, Richard, who may have been the first born; he died in 1796, a farmer from Myddle, and was buried at Baschurch.

---

60   *Calendar of Inquisitions miscellaneous (Chancery)*, I (1916), p101
61   University of Birmingham, Cadbury Research Library, Mytton Papers, V, p1001A-1002; J. Pryce-Jones, 'Oswestry Corporation records: the bailiffs from mediaeval times to 1673', *Trans. Shrops. Arch. & Hist. Soc.*, 76 (2001), p30-39; also 80 (2005), p190-192

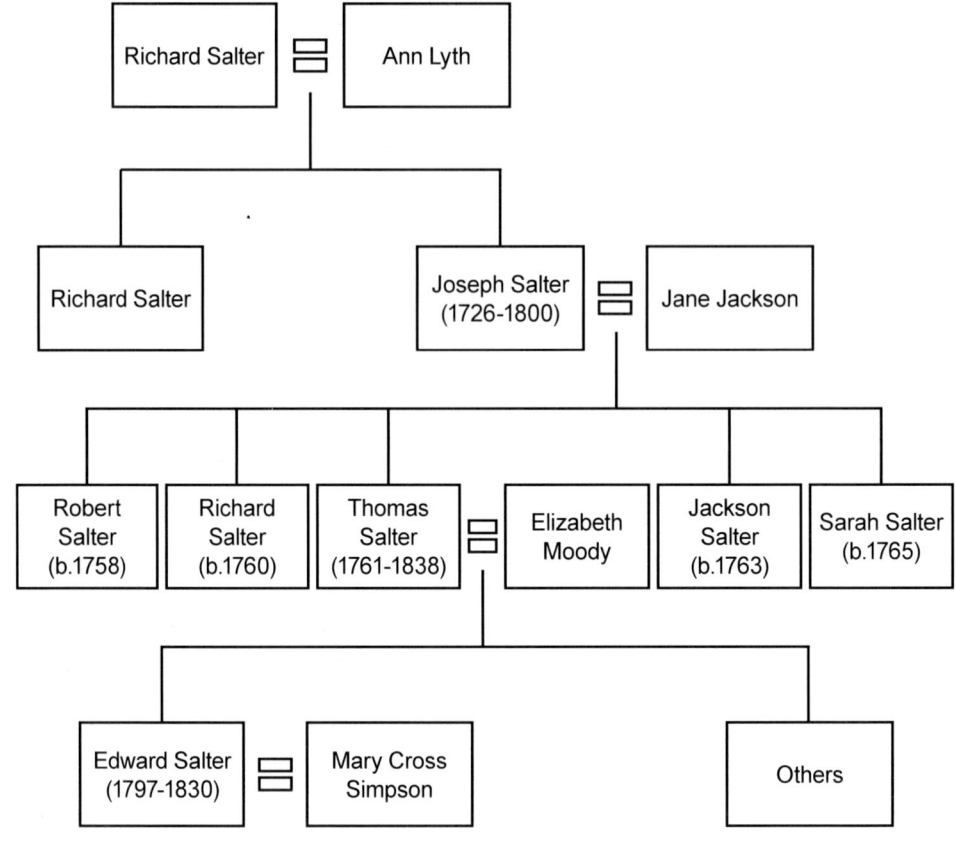

Wilfred Owen's ancestry: the Salter family.

Joseph Salter would have served the usual seven-year apprenticeship, to 1750. It is possible that he returned to live in Little Ness at some point since, in January 1758, when he married Jane Jackson of Ellesmere, at Ellesmere parish church, he is described as of the parish of Little Ness. Their first child, Robert, was baptised at Baschurch in November 1758, but the young family must have moved back to Oswestry soon afterwards as the remaining four children, Richard, Thomas, Jackson and Sarah, born between 1760 and 1765, were all baptised at St Oswald's. For the first three Oswestry baptisms, Joseph was described as a watchmaker, of Cross Street; for the last, in 1765, he was described as a clockmaker.

Sarah died aged 15, but the four sons all prospered. Robert, the eldest, followed his father into watch making and subsequently traded from premises in Bailey Street as a seedsman; Jackson became a successful printer; and Richard served in the Army, being described in 1814 in the parish registers as 'Gent', living in the Candy, and in 1816 as captain of the local militia. His monument in the churchyard, from 1849, names him as Captain Richard Salter, the Candy; one of his sons, a second Jackson, born in Londonderry when his father was serving in Ireland, was another printer and bookseller, and Mayor of Oswestry in 1866. Thomas Salter, the third son, born in 1761, became a successful Oswestry timber merchant; he was the father of Edward Salter, the builder of Plas Wilmot.

Joseph Salter had a long and successful life. Watchmaker, clockmaker, he also traded in timber, and had a portfolio of other business interests – including those of his sons. He served as churchwarden at St Oswald's in 1763. He died in 1800.

Thomas Salter married Elizabeth Moody at St Oswald's on August 7th 1792. Elizabeth was the daughter of Richard Moody, a shoemaker, and subsequently landlord of the Bell. Thomas Salter had premises at the rear of the public house, off Lower Brook Street, for his timber business. Thomas and Elizabeth had several children; Edward, their eldest son, was born in 1797. Thomas died in 1838, aged 77; his widow, Elizabeth, lived on to 1852, and was 79 years old at the time of her death.

Biographers have also focussed on Plas Wilmot as Wilfred Owen's birthplace, and on Edward Salter, the poet's great grandfather, as the builder of Plas Wilmot. Dominic Hibberd noted that "Edward trained as a joiner, no doubt under the supervision of his father the timber merchant and at an early age went to Chester to make his fortune". Generally, biographers have been silent in respect of Edward Salter's wife, Mary. Dominic Hibberd described her simply as a local girl, stating that Edward Salter had returned to Oswestry from Chester in 1820 "to marry a local girl, Mary Cross Simpson". It is not clear when exactly Edward Salter moved to Chester, though he was clearly living there at the time of his marriage, at Oswestry's parish church on November 17th 1820, the church register describing him as a bachelor of the parish of St Martin, Chester, with his bride, Mary Cross Simpson, listed as a spinster of the parish of Oswestry.

After the wedding, Edward returned to Chester with his wife Mary – and lived there for the remainder of his life, until his early death in January 1830. Edward and Mary's children were born in Chester between 1821 and 1829. Their daughter Mary was the first, born on September 3$^{rd}$ 1821 and baptised on February 6$^{th}$ 1822. In the baptism records for the children Edward was described as a joiner. For the christening of his first child, at St Mary's, Chester, the family's address was given as "Walls". The three younger children, Edward (sometimes known as Edwin), Harriet and Francis, were all baptised at Holy Trinity, Chester, with the family's address given as St Martin in the Fields, Chester.

Evidence from the *Chester Courant* of December 25$^{th}$ 1821 shows that "Mr Salter, builder" had contributed £20 to the subscription fund towards the £1,000 fine imposed by the Court of King's Bench on Alderman John Williamson, former Lord Mayor of Chester, the fine being "for corruption in the execution of his office" in relation to the 1820 elections. In August 1823, a report in the *Chester Courant* showed that Edward Salter, builder was a member of a grand jury assembled to hear cases before the Chester City Sessions. Other press reports indicate that he was also appointed to serve on the Grand Jury in 1825 and 1828, and was also involved in the running of the Chester House of Industry, as one of the elected Guardians of the Poor for St Martin's parish.

The *Chester Advertiser* of February 4$^{th}$ 1825 included a notice, headed "Handsome family cottage", in which Mr Salter, builder, advertised to be let "the comfortable and beautifully situated house, called Woodbine Cottage, in Eaton Road within the city of Chester, comprising every convenience for a small genteel family, with stable, coach-house and other convenient out offices", with three acres of land and "a large garden attached to the premises, well stocked with choice fruit trees". Might this have been Edward and Mary's own home; might it suggest that the family may have moved at around this time to St Martin's Fields, immediately to the west of the city centre, and within the walls?

In October 1826, the *Chester Chronicle* included a notice that "the partnership carried on in the city of Chester between John Williamson [presumably the former Mayor] and Edward Salter as carpenters under the firm of Williamson & Salter was dissolved by mutual consent on the twenty second day of October instant, and the business in future will be carried on by the said Mr John Williamson". Another notice, in the *Chester Chronicle* of September 7$^{th}$ 1827, announced that "Edward Salter carpenter and joiner respectfully informs his friends that he has commenced business in the above line in the Yard and Premises adjoining the Northgate, and hopes by the strictest attention to their orders to merit a share of their patronage and support". Clearly, in September 1827, Edward Salter was looking forward to a new business venture; in April 1828, he was elected, quite possibly re-elected, as one of the Guardians of the Poor; and in August 1828 he served again on the Grand Jury. It looks that Edward and Mary were setting down roots in Chester, with Edward Salter involved in city life. However, twelve months later, in July 1829, detailed preparations for the new house at Plas Wilmot were well underway, with construction works commenced by August of that year.

Details written in a notebook preserved in the local collection of Oswestry Library indicate that Edward Salter was closely involved in planning and supervising the building of Plas Wilmot. Headed 'Notebook giving details on the building of Plas Wilmot on Edward Salter's croft at Croes Wyllan 1829', this fascinating document includes lists of the labourers employed on the project, the carters paid for carrying building material to the site, and wages paid from August to December 1829. Turning the book around, and starting at the back, there is a copy of a memorandum of agreement between Edward Salter of Chester and James Payne of Oswestry, for the manufacture of 40,000 bricks on site; there are also agreements with Henry Evans of Oswestry to undertake the brickwork; Thomas Richards, carrier; Edward Evans, slater; Charles Miller of Oswestry, mason; Mr Stokes for plastering; and Mr Eyeley for painting. The notebook shows that slates came from Llanrhaeadr; lime from Coedygo; and stone from Sweeney Mountain.

However, on January 15th 1830, the *Chester Chronicle* reported Edward Salter's death. He had died on January 10th, "after a long illness", at the age of only 32. Work on Plas Wilmot had commenced in August 1829; at the time of Edward's death it is likely that it was still unfinished, still in need of completion and fitting out. Had the new house been planned by Edward Salter for an early retirement, or at least a period of recuperation after his long period of illness, or was it perhaps built in the knowledge that Edward might not have had long to live, as a home for his young family to return to? Edward had died leaving his wife Mary, aged only 30, with four children to look after, the eldest 8 years old, the youngest, Francis, only 2 months old and christened on January 28th, less than 3 weeks after his father's funeral in Chester.

We have seen that Mary Salter, formerly Mary Cross Simpson, was described in the marriage register as being "of the parish", and therefore taken by biographers to be a local girl. However, although she was living in the parish in 1820, evidence will show that she was not particularly local.

Mary was the daughter of Mary Cross Cowper Simpson. She died in 1842, aged forty two, her name, "Mary relict of the late Edward Salter of Chester", being engraved on a monument formerly in the churchyard of St Oswald's alongside the names of her mother "Mary Cross Cowper relict of C.C. Simpson of Worcester" and Harriet Salkeld[62]; the three ladies being listed in the 1841 Census as the residents of Plas Wilmot, along with Mary Salter's daughter Mary and a domestic servant. It seems likely that Mary moved to Oswestry with her mother at some point between 1815 and 1820. It is not clear why mother and daughter chose to settle in Oswestry, but records show that other individuals and families with the income to support a comfortable lifestyle were moving to the town and the district at this time. A brief report in the *Morning Post*, for July 22nd 1815 headed 'Fashionable departures' records the departure, I believe from London, "for Oswestry, Salop" of "Mr and Miss Simpson", likely to be a misprint for "*Mrs* and Miss Simpson". If mother and daughter did indeed arrive in Oswestry in July 1815, Mary would have been around 15 years old, and her mother Mrs Cross Simpson around 47 or 48. The husband and father, Mr Simpson, had died in May 1815. The *Salisbury & Winchester Journal* for May 15th reported that "On Thursday last William Simpson Esquire of Berwick St John died at his lodgings in this city" [Salisbury]. Other newspapers of the time, and also the monthly *Gentleman's Magazine*, reported the death of "William Cross Simpson, Esquire, formerly a banker of Worcester". His body was buried at Salisbury Cathedral: records confirm that there was a flat gravestone on the south side of the cathedral cloisters, with cathedral registers recording the burial of William C.C. Simpson, amended to William Cross Simpson, 48, of Berwick St James, on May 18th; he had died on May 11th 1815.

---

62   'Oswestry old church monuments', *Trans. Shrops. Arch. Soc.*, 6 (1883), p157

Tracing Wilfred Owen's family background back beyond William Cross Simpson and his wife Mary proved a challenge. There seemed to be too many surnames to work with – Simpson, Cross and also the name Cowper. However, the will of Mary Cross Cowper Simpson, who died in 1844, proved to be helpful, referring as it did to her grand-daughters Mary and Harriet Salter and grandsons Edwin and Francis Salter, as well as to Harriet Salkeld, and to her own late mother Mary Fewtrell of Worcester. In turn, Mary Fewtrell's will[63], of 1814, referring as it did to her daughter Mary as the "wife of William Cross Simpson Esquire", provided further confirmation.

Turning to the third of the three ladies living at Plas Wilmot in 1841, Harriet Salkeld, the question still to be answered was how exactly was she related to the Salters, or to the Cross Simpsons. The 1851 Census helped, listing at Plas Wilmot the 29 year old Mary Salter as head of household, ahead of Harriet Salkeld, of independent means, with the latter's birthplace given as Shrewsbury. Other references to Salkelds in Worcester and in Shrewsbury were then found, and also the will of Hannah Salkeld[64], a tea dealer, who died in 1817 in Shrewsbury, her will referring to children including a daughter Harriet. The marriage, at old St Chad's, Shrewsbury, in August 1770, of William Salkeld and Hannah Cross of the parish of St Alkmund's, provided the explanation for Harriet Salkeld's connection to Mary Cross Simpson and her daughter. Harriet was William and Hannah's first child, born in Shrewsbury in 1771 or thereabouts. An advertisement in the *Shrewsbury Chronicle* for May 25th 1776 showed that William Salkeld had business ties with Thomas Cross, wine merchant, of Ludlow, samples of whose Herefordshire cider could be tasted at Salkeld's coffee house on Pride Hill. William Salkeld was Thomas Cross' son-in-law, as his wife Hannah was the wine merchant's daughter.

---

63  National Archives, PROB 11/1580/121
64  National Archives, PROB 11/1598/145

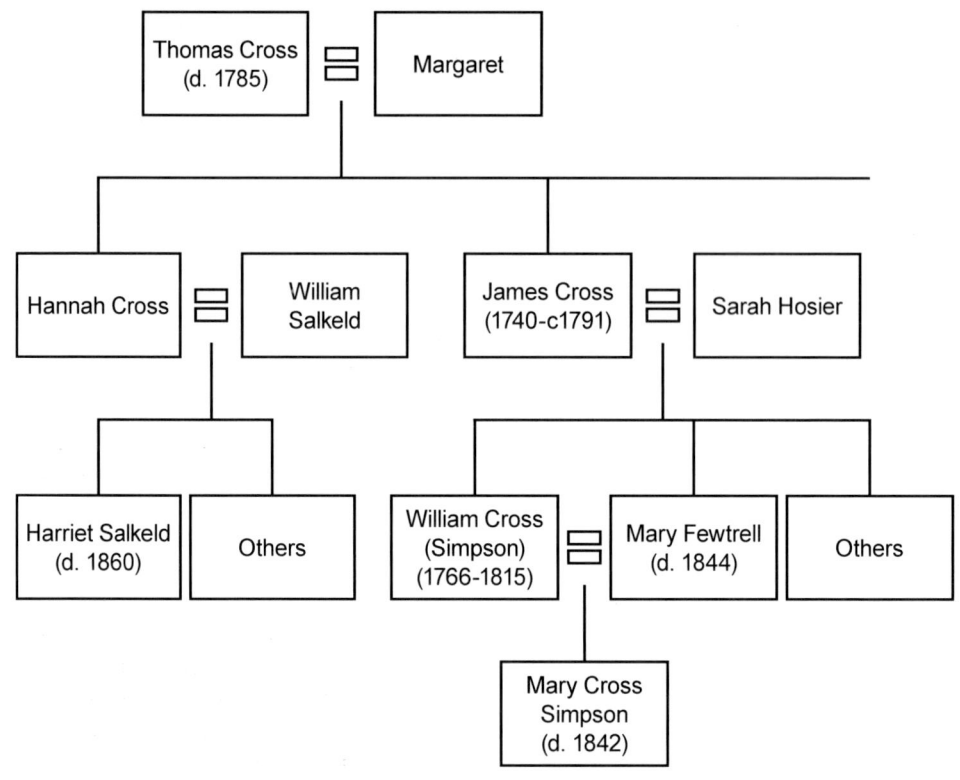

Wilfred Owen's ancestry: the Cross family.

A visit to Worcestershire Archives provided details of the marriage on July 20th 1786, at St Nicholas' church in Foregate Street, Worcester, of Mary Fewtrell, spinster, of the parish of St Nicholas, and William Cross, bachelor, of the parish of Clifton, in the county of Gloucester[65]. Comparing these details with those in Mary Cross Cowper Simpson's will of 1843, and her mother Mary Fewtrell's will of 1814, confirmed that William Cross of Clifton and William Cross Simpson Esquire were the same man.

---

65 The witnesses included Mary's mother, another Mary Fewtrell, and James Cross (either William's father, or his brother) and Robert Kyrle Hutcheson, William's brother in law

Contemporary newspaper reports include several references to William Cross's business dealings[66]. These were not always entirely successful: a banking business, in Worcester, in Ledbury, and also in Lombard Street in the city of London; and a wine merchant's in Tewkesbury all appear to have failed during the financial crisis of 1793, leading to the dissolution of partnerships, and several years of creditor meetings and court action, reported in the local press, and in the *London Gazette*. For example, the *Hereford Journal* of June 26th 1793 included a notice alerting readers to the dissolution of the partnership behind a bank known as Hankins, Mutlow, Cross, Embury and Glover. Likewise, the same newspaper for October 11th 1797 included a notice pursuant to a court order issued against Joseph Glover, William Edwards, William Cross and John Embury, bankers of Worcester.

The will of William's father James Cross, distiller, of Clifton, dated 1786, with a codicil of 1788, is preserved at the National Archives in Kew, the will being proved in July 1791[67]. The will includes reference to James Cross' business interests in distilling, and in brewing, maltings, and wholesale spirits, in both Bristol and Bath, and includes a description of his new house in Clifton, with grounds, gardens, orchards, hot houses, a coach house and stables, recently purchased from Edward Elton of the city of Bristol. William Cross was mentioned in his father's will as one of a number of men with whom James was involved in the distillery business, but William's bequest was changed by a codicil so that he would be paid a 'lump sum' of £3,000 within two years of his father's death rather than having an equal share with his siblings in his father's estate, the £3,000 to be paid less deductions of any sums of money already advanced or to be advanced to his son "for his promotion in the world".

James Cross' will named his wife Sarah, and his sister in law Ann Hosier, providing the link back to Ludlow, where the registers for St Lawrence's for November 20th 1762 recorded the marriage of James Cross and Sarah Hosier. Ludlow's parish registers provided details of James and Sarah's children: Thomas, baptised in 1763, who died in infancy, Sarah (1764), James (1765), William (1766), and a second Thomas (1768). Other children were born after the family's move to Bristol, which seems to have taken place in the year or so following the second Thomas' baptism. It seems very likely that the distiller James Cross was born in Ludlow in 1740, son of Thomas Cross, wine merchant and his wife Margaret. As noted, Thomas had family ties to William Salkeld of Shrewsbury[68].

---

66   Details obtained by use of the online resource the British Newspaper Archive
67   National Archives, PROB 11/1206/310
68   Thomas Cross may also have done some distilling: there are Ludlow deeds from this time which suggest this, and refer to stills at premises in Mill Street

Summing up, it seems that James Cross, the son of a successful Ludlow wine merchant, moved south to Bristol with his wife Sarah and their young family and developed significant interests of his own in the distilling and brewing businesses. Their son William, who was living in the parish of Clifton in 1786 at the time of his marriage, appears then to have moved to Worcester, where he became a partner in a local bank[69]. His home, from 1792, possibly earlier, was Thorngrove, and he appears to have remained there until the turn of the century, the house being put up for sale in 1801. An advertisement in the *Gloucester Journal* of July 13th 1801 indicates that "the capital and commodious mansion house called Thorngrove situated in the Parish of Grimley", three miles from Worcester, was to be sold "by order of the High Court of Chancery" in relation to bankruptcy proceedings against "Joseph Glover, William Edwards, John Embury and William Cross, late of the city of Worcester, bankers, bankrupts". The house was "delightfully situated on an eminence commanding a view of the River Severn and a beautiful prospect over the most fertile country terminated on the south west by the grand and much-admired range of Malvern Hills, and on the north by the more picturesque one of Abberley". The house had "five rooms on a floor, the dining room being 33 feet 6 inches by 20 feet 7 inches, the drawing room 20 feet by 16, and other rooms of large dimensions, with closets, cold and hot baths". There were stables, a coach house, malt-house, hop-kilns, outbuildings, as well as pleasure grounds and shrubbery walks, a large kitchen garden, and a "circular stone-built gothic green-house", the house being set in 130 acres of grounds[70].

William Cross, his wife Mary and their infant daughter (Mary, who married Edward Salter), had to move elsewhere. In 1807 William's address was Leith Vale, a substantial house with grounds on the Surrey/Sussex border, and at the time of his death in 1815, he was living in Berwick St James north of Salisbury. Clearly the family were used to fine living.

---

69  *London Gazette*, 11 February 1792, includes a notice dated 10 December 1791, indicating changes in the partnership, from one of Joseph Glover, Samuel Edwards, John Embury, William Cross and Thomas Benbow, so that Samuel Edwards was replaced by William Edwards

70  In July 1811, Thorngrove was home to Lucien Bonaparte, Napoleon's younger brother, captured by the Royal Navy in 1810, and allowed to live in some luxury in England – first at Ludlow, then at Thorngrove. Later it was home to the African explorer Sir Samuel Baker.

The name Simpson remained a puzzle, ultimately solved by a notice in the *London Gazette* for April 28th 1807 announcing that king George III had been pleased to grant unto William Cross of Leith Vale, in the county of Sussex, and of Lincoln's Inn, esquire, student of law, eldest surviving son and heir of James Cross, late of Clifton, "his royal licence and authority that he and his issue may assume and take the surnames of Cowper Simpson in addition to his present surname of Cross, and that he and they may bear the Arms of Simpson quarterly with those of Cross" this change being "in compliance with the desire of John Simpson of Westgate House, near Louth, in the county of Lincoln … from the particular esteem and affection which he has long borne for the said William Cross and being himself without children". A report in the *Stamford Mercury* confirmed that John Simpson was "a West Indian merchant" and had at one time been Member of Parliament for the borough of St Michael's in Cornwall[71]. Westgate House was described as "lately erected, altered and improved under the minutest inspection and direction of an eminent surveyor" containing "numerous large lofty well-proportioned rooms" including "a spacious entrance hall" approached by a double flight of stone stairs, a breakfast and tea room, drawing room, dining room "communicating by large mahogany folding doors", a saloon decorated with views of the Isle of Wight "designed and executed by that ingenious artist Mr Murant of Ludgate Hill", and a large

Westgate House, Louth, the Lincolnshire home of the merchant John Simpson, benefactor to William Cross.
Photograph © John Pryce-Jones.

---

71  *Stamford Mercury*, 13 January 1809

library room, along with "excellent arched cellars"[72]. Like William Cross, John Simpson had his financial problems, forcing him to sell up in Louth – his house, other lands, and the contents of his wine cellars – and to move to London. Like William Cross, he had at one point been a partner in a bank, in his case in Southampton. Where and when he had come into contact with William Cross is not clear; it is possible that they had links through their business interests.

Finally, then to Mary Fewtrell, who married William Cross in 1786, and who became Mary Cross Cowper Simpson in 1807. Born in 1767 or 1768 in Worcester, her father was James Fewtrell, innkeeper, of the Hop Pole in Foregate Street. The Hop Pole was one of the city's foremost inns – used, like the Wynnstay in Oswestry, for public meetings[73], auctions and celebratory dinners. Nelson stayed at the Hop Pole when he visited Worcester in 1802. James Fewtrell was a man of some influence in Worcester: he was treasurer to the commissioners appointed to provide a water supply, better paving and lighting for the city, and in that role, he gave evidence to Parliament in 1780. He died in 1782.

Her mother was another Mary who as Mary Woodcock had married James Fewtrell on June 27th 1766 at the church of St Marylebone, Middlesex. James was Mary's second husband; as Mary Morris, she had married George Woodcock of Worcester in 1760. George Woodcock had died in February 1762, leaving to his brother the Rev. John Woodcock the "inn in Foregate Street now in my own occupation and which was heretofore three dwelling houses and called the Hop Pole which I hold by lease under the Dean and Chapter of Worcester", reserving a life interest to his wife[74]. The Reverend Mr Woodcock died in 1781; he was outlived by his sister in law by thirty five years: the widow Mary Fewtrell was ninety seven years old at her death in 1816.

---

72  *Stamford Mercury*, 18 May 1810
73  Including, in 1797, a meeting of the creditors of William Cross
74  George Woodcock's will is available at Worcestershire Archives

It is interesting to note, from generation to generation, from will to will, from Mary Fewtrell through to Mary Cross Cowper Simpson and on to Mary Salter, a common thread of seeking to protect the interests of the daughters of the family. In James Fewtrell's will[75], prepared in 1780 and witnessed by John Woodcock, he made arrangements for his wife Mary to receive £200 a year over and above the sum mentioned in the marriage settlement for the remainder of her life, so long as she did not remarry, with the residue to his daughter Mary (the future Mary Cross Cowper Simpson) once she reached the age of 21. In Mary Fewtrell's will, drawn up in 1814, and proved in 1816, the previous marriage settlement, set out in an indenture of 1776, is set out – she was to have "a power of disposition of the sum of one thousand pounds". Her will was very detailed, and set out how Charles Thompson of Lincoln's Inn, and two Worcester bankers William Wall and Elias Isaac were to be entrusted with the £1000 and the remainder of Mary Fewtrell's personal estate to be invested in Government securities so as to provide an income for her daughter. These payments were be made "to my daughter only for her own sole separate use free from the control debts or engagements & intermeddling of her present or any after taken husband" – bearing in mind that William Cross Simpson was still alive when the will was prepared - and after her daughter's death were to be paid to her grandchildren, in fact to her grand daughter Mary, the future Mary Salter. Finally, Mary Cross Cowper Simpson's will, drafted in 1843 and proved in 1844, followed the same pattern, rehearsing her mother's will, and appointing a solicitor George Salter of Ellesmere to look after the trust monies for the benefit of her two grand-daughters Harriet and Mary Salter – her daughter Mary Salter having died in 1842. Her two grandsons Edwin and Francis Salter were provided with separate bequests on condition that their sisters were permitted to continue to live at Plas Wilmot.

These arrangements, and the sums involved, may cast some doubt upon the idea that Edward Salter built and paid for Plas Wilmot having "made his fortune" in Chester. Would Edward Salter have had the means to develop Plas Wilmot? He died young, aged only 32: would he have had time to make his fortune in Chester? Might he have needed assistance from others, notably from his wife Mary and her mother Mary Cross Cowper Simpson? It is clear that Edward Salter's wife Mary came from a family background where she would have been used to fine living, and elegant houses. I believe there is a strong possibility that it was money from Mary Salter's family that financed, or significantly contributed to, the costs of building and running Plas Wilmot and, prior to that, to the costs of Edward and Mary's family home in Chester. It is interesting to note, in Edward Salter's will, that he described his mother in law Mary Cross Cowper Simpson as "my kind friend", making her and his wife Mary Salter joint executrices of his will and guardians of his children.

---

75  National Archives, PROB 11/1097/50

As a young widow and mother, with four young children, it seems that Mary Salter was joined at Plas Wilmot by her mother Mary Simpson and, at some point before 1841, by Harriet Salkeld[76], the daughter of Hannah Cross and therefore a cousin of William Cross Simpson. Plas Wilmot had also been the home of Mrs Ann Bourke, widow of the Rev. J.W. Bourke, vicar of St Oswald's[77], for a short time prior to her death in October 1833.

In conclusion, and returning to Wilfred Owen, it may be that his family history did not link back to the mediaeval Salters of Oswestry; nevertheless, his Salter ancestors had made their mark on Oswestry in the 18th and 19th centuries. Wilfred was well aware of his Salter heritage – he had been given Salter as a middle name. He may though have been less aware, or unaware, of his ancestors from the Cross and the Fewtrell families, in Ludlow, Shrewsbury, Worcester, and Bristol, and of the role that those ancestors may have had in the creation of Plas Wilmot.

*Based on articles printed in St Oswald's Parish Magazine for April and May 2015, and very largely on a talk given to the Oswestry and Border History and Archaeology Group (OBHAG) on March 10th 2017*

---

76 Harriet Salkeld's will survives; one of her executors was Mary Shaw, the former Mary Salter, with whom she would have shared Plas Wilmot for the last 30 years of her life. Given the early deaths of Mary's parents Edward and Mary Salter, and then of her grandmother Mary Simpson in 1844, it is likely that Mary and the other Salter children would have seen Harriet Salkeld as an important link to their parents, and to their own childhoods

77 He was vicar of Oswestry from 1807 until his death in 1823

## Chapter 24: Football crazy, football mad

It is well known that churches and chapels played an important part in the development of a number of major English football clubs, including Everton, Manchester City and Aston Villa. Each began when a local church formed a football team in order to provide what was thought to be a wholesome, and a healthy pursuit for young men, and an alternative to the evils of drink.

The modern laws of association football were agreed in 1863, enabling football to become more organised, less a random free-for-all kickabout. The game grew rapidly in popularity in the 1860s and 1870s, with the then ever-expanding railway network enabling travel between towns and villages for matches. In Oswestry, it is known that the local club was one of the founders of the Welsh Football Association in 1876 and provided nine of the eleven members of the Welsh team when Wales first played England, in 1879. It has been claimed that the town club was formed as early as 1860, making it one of the oldest clubs in the country, but whilst it is the case that organised football can indeed be traced back in Oswestry into the 1860s, the Oswestry club was actually formed on September 4th 1875 at a public meeting held at the Queen's Hotel.

However, the town club was not the first team to be formed in Oswestry. Football matches were played by Oswestry School as early as 1866, and the role of St Oswald's parish church in these early years of local, and Welsh football more generally, can be traced back to January 1870 when a branch of the Church of England Young Men's Society was established. The *Advertizer* reported throughout that year on the society's meetings, which were held at the Victoria Rooms, but it is not clear precisely when the Young Men's Society established a football team.

The earliest surviving reference to a church football team dates from 1871, when on November 18th 1871 a match was held between Oswestry St Oswald's and Whittington, on the latter's pitch. The *Advertizer* listed both sides in full (there were sixteen players recorded on each side!); the St Oswald's team comprised, in no particular order: Wynne (captain), Cartwright, Cuthbert, W.H. Davies, Evans, Glascodine, Gough, Higham, Lloyd, Mitchell, Pugh, Saunders, W. Shepherd, Thomas, H. Williams, and T.F. Williams. It seems likely that 'Cuthbert' would have been one of the sons of the Rev. George Cuthbert, then the senior curate at St Oswald's. The players were generally in their mid-teens: in 1871 George Glascodine, the son of an auctioneer's clerk, was fourteen years old, William Henry Davies, a hatter's son, fifteen, W.H. Gough, whose father was George Gough, superintendent of the Police, eighteen, and George Higham, the son of gunmaker Samuel Higham, was fifteen.

The *Parish Magazine* for December 1872 reported that the club met for practice every Saturday at 2.30, "in a field at Old Oswestry kindly lent by Mr Owen of the Oldport". Over the next four or five years the St Oswald's club built up a programme of 'friendly' fixtures against other local teams including Oswestry Grammar School, the Ruabon club, Wrexham, Whittington, and All Saints (Shrewsbury). In December 1874 and January 1875 St Oswald's played home and away against Plasmadoc (the forerunner of the renowned Druids), winning 1-0 at home, and losing away by the same score. Clearly, they were a strong side, and a force to be reckoned with.

We have seen that a 'Town Club' was formed in September 1875. For the St Oswald's team this had unfortunate consequences, resulting as it did in the loss of several key players. The Town Club may have had greater resources, and certainly was able to develop a more ambitious fixture list which by the early 1880s included matches against the likes of Wolverhampton Wanderers, Stoke, Aston Villa and Crewe. That said, as the church team had been established specifically for young men and teenagers, it was perhaps right that its players should move on to other local clubs, providing scope for the next cohort of younger boys to come through. In any event, by the end of 1875, founder members of the St Oswald's team including the goalkeeper Glascodine, the forward Davies and the back Higham were regulars in the Town side. Indeed, all three went on to represent Wales: they all played in that famous first fixture against England in January 1879. Oswestry's W.H. Davies scored Wales' first ever international goal in that same match.

*Based on an article printed in St Oswald's Parish Magazine for November 2014*

# Chapter 25: George Bonner, artist and engraver

The website Art UK (www.artuk.org) formerly known as 'Your paintings' and established through a partnership between the BBC and the charity the Public Catalogue Foundation is well known. Featured in BBC programmes such as *Britain's lost masterpieces*, the project seeks to make more widely available art housed in galleries and museums, on display and in store, along with paintings and the like owned by other bodies such as universities and colleges, or displayed in hospitals, town halls and other civic buildings. Currently the site includes details of works of art held by over 3,000 UK institutions, and includes digital images of over 230,000 art works by over 40,000 artists.

The site is searchable, by institution, by artist, and by subject. Users can search for Oswestry Town Council and will be presented with images of fourteen paintings held at the Guildhall, the majority of these being portraits of former Mayors from the 18th and 19th centuries. They can choose to search using the search term 'Shropshire' to identify the 210 paintings included on the site which relate, in some way, to Shropshire, or search for 'Oswestry' which will bring up 19 works relating to Oswestry, in some way, including just three paintings on the system actually depicting Oswestry.

One of those three paintings is that painted by William Williams in 1779, portraying Church Street, looking towards the New Gate and town centre[78]. This is not the subject of this essay: its focus is rather on the other two paintings. Of those two, the one is listed on the Art UK website as 'The Guildhall, Oswestry', dated to 1890, and painted by 'G. Bonner'. The other, given the title 'Bailey Head, Oswestry, Shropshire' and dated on the site to 1883, is listed as 'by an unknown artist'. However, reports from the *Advertizer* confirm that this painting dates to 1888 or 1889, and was also by Mr Bonner. The *Advertizer* for January 9th 1889 reported that, at that time, the painting was on display at Mr Owen's, the Library, Oswestry (the premises at the corner of Leg Street and Cross Street, now the British Red Cross' shop premises). Two weeks later, the *'Tizer* for January 23rd included an advertisement announcing that the "large oil painting by George Bonner" entitled 'Fair Day on the Bailey Head, Oswestry' could "now be seen in the window of Messrs Jones and Roberts, confectioners, Bailey Street".

---

78  The painting is featured on the front cover of *An Oswestry miscellany* (2007)

Readers of the *Advertizer* were advised that "Mr George Bonner of Beatrice Street has completed a large and elaborate oil painting he has been engaged upon for the last twelve months", the reporter describing how "the point of view from which the picture is taken is the corner of Albion Hill and Bailey Street. The Powis Hall and the Guildhall are carefully and accurately drawn, so that in years to come when the Guildhall, at any rate, will have been replaced by a building more worthy of the town of Oswestry, the picture will have a historic interest. The amount of labour expended upon the painting may be judged of from the fact that it contains two hundred figures, including portraits of well known inhabitants of Oswestry and the neighbourhood". The report concluded by saying that "the picture is now on view and is for sale".

So, who was George Bonner? Records confirm that George Frederick Bonner lived in Oswestry and district from around 1878 or 1879 through until his death, aged 72, in May 1896. He was born in 1823, in Newington, Surrey, south of the Thames in London. His parents were the artist and engraver George Wilmot Bonner (1796-1836) and his wife Sophia. Brought up in Newington, he was described in the 1841 Census as an engraver, learning the trade from his mother alongside two apprentices. However, in May 1848 at the time of his marriage to Susanna Sharpe, a farmer's daughter, in Gloucestershire, he was listed as a cabinet maker, though, later the same year, then described as an 'upholsterer, cabinet maker, dealer and chapman' of Cheltenham, he was declared bankrupt. At the time of the 1851 Census, George, now described as an engraver in wood, and Susanna were still living in Cheltenham, with their infant son, but by the end of 1851, when their second child was born, they were back in Newington. Over the thirty years of their marriage, George and Susanna moved home a number of times, mainly within London, and had seven children: George, Sophia, Laura, William, Alice, Florence and Frances.

Trained as an engraver by his parents, the 1861 Census described him as an 'artist and engraver in wood'; in the 1871 Census he was an 'engraver and printer'. At his death in 1896, local newspapers noted how, during his time in London, he had been "engaged on the staff of the *Illustrated London News*, the *Graphic*, and *Reynolds' Newspaper*", three of the major titles of the time, all three pioneers in the use of illustrations as a means of reporting the news. Whether he was taken on by these 'papers as an employee is unclear – he may have worked as a freelance, employed as and when his skills as an artist and engraver were required.

Certainly, he had business interests of his own, though records indicate that his ventures were not always successful ones. In 1853 a partnership with Joseph Benwell as 'designers, lithographers and wood engravers' was dissolved by mutual consent; in 1860, he was listed in the *London Gazette* as one of a number of people who had petitioned the Court for Relief of Insolvent Debtors, and had obtained an interim order protecting them from process, and who were required to appear before the court, in Lincoln's Inn, to be examined. The listing gives Bonner's address at that time – 2 Elizabeth Terrace, Homerton, renting an office at 34 Bouverie Street (off Fleet Street) - and notes three former addresses, in Kingsland (Hackney), Walworth and Newington Butts. In 1866 the *London Gazette* recorded that bankruptcy had been awarded against George Frederick Bonner "of 4 Lower Searles Place, Temple Bar and of 4 Norton Cottages, Malden Crescent, Haverstock Hill, printer, formerly of 90 Islip Street, Kentish Town, manager at the office of *Reynolds' Newspaper*". Finally, in 1871, the *Gazette* listed a meeting of the creditors of Mr Bonner, now of 6 Molesworth Street, Lewisham, to be held in relation to proceedings brought by Bonner "for liquidation by arrangement or composition with creditors".

His wife Susanna died in March 1878, in Lewisham.

George Bonner first appears in Oswestry's local records in 1879. The Post Office Directory for 1879 listed George Bonner, described as a photographer, at an address in Oswald Road. Also, the *Advertizer* for July 23$^{rd}$ 1879 included a notice announcing the marriage at Llanymynech of George Bonner and a Miss E. Humphreys. Later that year, an advertisement appeared in the local press: "REQUIRED for the St Martins Coffee House and Reading Rooms, a MAN and WIFE, without children. Must have good characters. The house is furnished, rent free, coals and lights provided. The Manager to receive profits from the sales. Apply, with all particulars (by letter), to Mr J. EDWARDS, Tailor, St Martins, Chirk". Details from October 1880 of a case determined at the County Court, brought against George Bonner by the Right Honourable Lord Trevor, of Brynkinallt, indicates that Mr Bonner had applied for the vacant post, and managed the Coffee House, a temperance house, from January to April 1880. Lord Trevor took the matter to court seeking unpaid rent of £2 3s 11d. In response, Mr Bonner claimed a loss of £13 17s 3d for loss incurred through the "alleged misrepresentation on the part of Lady Trevor" as to the takings of the Coffee House; he also claimed that there was no water within a quarter mile of the house and that he had to pay someone to have water carried from a well. The case was decided in favour of Lord Trevor: Mr Bonner was required to pay the rent in three monthly instalments, the judge, in making his decision, leaving open a possible claim by Bonner for the £13 loss. It is not clear whether this was pursued.

In 1881, at the time of the next ten-yearly Census, Mr & Mrs Bonner were living at Ifton Heath, he was then 57, his second wife Elizabeth (born in Llansantffraid) was 31. He was listed this time as 'artist, engraver in wood and photographer'. They must have moved back to the town of Oswestry shortly afterwards. By 1884 Bonner was operating in partnership with a Mr Sneyd as Bonner & Sneyd from premises at 57 Willow Street. In August 1884 they placed advertisements in local newspapers including those for Shrewsbury and Wrexham promoting the sale of "a magnificent picture" to be produced in limited numbers "in the highest style of art exquisitely printed in chromo-lithography" of the Williams Wynns, including views of such places as Wynnstay, Llangedwyn Hall and Ruabon Church. However, the partnership appears to have been short-lived as by 1885 a local trade directory listed Mr Bonner, without any partner, in Beatrice Street, as an engraver. Six years on, the *Advertizer* reported that "an office for the receipt of letters, parcels &c will shortly be opened at the shop of Mr G. Bonner, photographer and engraver, Beatrice Street". The 1891 Census confirms that their address at this time was 36 Beatrice Street.

Returning to the paintings, it is probably reasonable to consider that Mr Bonner produced them to raise additional household income, seeing local views as something that would generate local interest, and ready buyers for the works. Mr Bonner was "well known in the Masonic world in Shropshire" and for many years served as tyler (someone appointed to prepare the room for meetings, to guard the door, and to ensure that candidates for ceremonies in the Lodge are properly prepared) for both the FitzAlan and the St Oswald Masonic Lodges in Oswestry. Press reports noted that "He was most attentive and assiduous in his duties, and had well earned the respect and regard of the members of both lodges as well as of many prominent Freemasons in the province". Such a role would have provided him with numerous acquaintances and contacts, potential buyers for his works.

Each new picture was reported upon in the *Advertizer.*

Coverage in the *Advertizers* for January 1889 of the painting 'Fair Day on the Bailey Head', one of the two Bonner pictures owned by the Town Council, has already been noted.

In June 1889, the *Advertizer* in a detailed report on the Trefonen Eisteddfod noted that Bonner had submitted a painting of the Llwyd Mansion, it being the sole entry to a painting competition with a prize of ten shillings. He won the prize, though the praise of the judge, Colonel Barnes of Brookside, was not particularly fulsome: in a speech interspersed by laughter, he said that "it was not until that afternoon that he [had seen] the piece of work. He should say it was not a perfect work of art, for instance one did not quite know if the near side wheel of the 'bus in the picture was going to come off and upset the 'bus or not" continuing to say that "the artist had done his best to make a likeness of Mr Dumville Lees [of Woodhill, the appointed president for the day's events] but next time he must try to mount him on a superior steed to that on which he was represented as riding ... for the master of the Tanatside Hounds was known to possess an excellent stud of horses". However, the Colonel praised the depiction of Llwyd Mansion itself, concluding that "he hoped the artist would not be discouraged by his remarks".

In July 1889, a month later, the *Advertizer* reported another painting "now on view at Messrs R. and R. Hughes's in the Cross". Entitled 'A summer's evening on the Wynnstay green', the *Advertizer* noted that "it represents the Wynnstay Bowling Green ... with several well known local bowlers, and the fine tower of the old church rising in the background" commenting that "the view of the well known hotel and the tower which are faithfully reproduced, and the green and the group of players makes up a picture which will be still more interesting in years to come" adding that "one of our readers may like to secure it".

Next, in June 1890, Mr Bonner turned to Christ Church. The *Advertizer* reported, on June 11th, that the artist had "added another to his series of oil paintings of Oswestry scenes" noting that "in the opinion of some of those who have seen it, it is his best". On display at the premises of Messrs Woodall, Minshall & Co. on the Bailey Head, it was "a view of Christ Church from the Powis Hall end of the old Pitcher Bank. The surroundings are relieved by the introduction of some of the foliage of the Castle Bank and the ornamental ground and fountains which form part of the Castle Bank improvement scheme".

Finally, Bonner's painting of the old Guildhall, the second of the paintings owned by the Town Council, was described by the *'Tizer* on November 5th 1890: "the subject this time is the Bailey Head with a full view of the facade of the Guildhall, and the old buildings on both sides of it. The painting is a faithful picture, and when the building is replaced by the new municipal buildings [the present Guildhall, built in 1892] it will have historic interest to Oswestrians".

The Guildhall and Bailey Head (1890), a painting by G.F. Bonner. To the left is the Savings Bank, and to the right a glimpse of the Castle Bank and Powis market hall. Reproduced with permission of Oswestry Town Council.

George Bonner died six years later on May 10$^{th}$ 1896, aged 72; burial took place on May 12$^{th}$ at Oswestry's cemetery. His widow Elizabeth stayed on at 36 Beatrice Street, establishing a servants' registry office (a domestic service employment agency) there by 1900, a business which continued into the mid-1920s. She died in 1928, aged 80.

A number of questions remain. Further work in the Town Council archives at the Guildhall may establish precisely when the two Bonner paintings were acquired, and – if purchased - what the Town Council paid for them. Turning to the earlier of the two paintings, 'Fair Day on the Bailey Head, Oswestry', it would be interesting to see how many of the "well known inhabitants of Oswestry and the neighbourhood" might be identified by comparison with other portraits and photographs that may survive. This would be quite a challenge.

Finally, it would be good to be able to locate these other paintings by Bonner of local views – his painting of the Llwyd Mansion, with Mr Dumville Lees astride a horse; his depiction of Christ Church; and his view of the Wynnstay bowling green. It is likely that they survive, hanging in someone's house, or decorating an office wall. And it is possible that there were other paintings, which may also have survived. George Bonner was described in his obituaries as "the painter of several pictures of local interest", there may well have been more than just the five such paintings described here and it would be good for our local history to be able to bring all of these to light, as an important glimpse of Oswestry in late Victorian times.

# Chapter 26: What's in a house name?

Whilst place names, field names and street names have all received attention from historians and other students at a local and national level, there has been much less attention given to house names. It has been suggested that whilst the custom of personalising domestic properties with house names is a familiar one, "these house names have attracted little or no scholarly investigation"[79]. Perhaps this is because, compared to place names, house names can be more ephemeral, sometimes prone to cliché, and sometimes a little corny. Nevertheless, the study of Oswestry, the use of street directories and of Census returns, shows how some house names have remained unchanged, some throughout their life, whilst others have changed, once or several times. Further study has shown that some names have even 'moved' from one house to another, taken by their owners or tenants along with their furniture and fittings, when they have moved on to a new home elsewhere.

The idea of naming houses pre-dates the expansion of towns and cities; it reflects the established practice of the landed gentry in giving names to their homes and estates. The position in Oswestry and district was similar to that elsewhere in Shropshire or in the country generally. Prior to the late 18th century, country houses and farms had names which simply reflected their location – for example, Aston Hall, Brogyntyn Hall (then known as Porkington), Sweeney Hall and Llanforda Hall. However, by the late 18th century, and throughout the 19th century these long-established houses were joined in the local countryside by newer properties, often built for people new to the area, or for those had made money through, for instance, commerce or industry, the law or banking. These homes, planted into an existing landscape, had names chosen for them, names such as Woodhill in Trefonen; Mount Sion, later replaced by Oakhurst, on the road to Selattyn; Belmont (later Henlle Hall) near Gobowen; Plas Wilmot on Weston Lane; Belle Vue (later Glentworth) above the river Morda; and the later Beechfield and High Lea, both on the western outskirts of Oswestry.

---

79  *Friends of the Centre for English Local History*, 23 (October 2010), p7, a review of a lecture by Dr Christopher Lewis on 1920s and 1930s house names on the Sussex coast.

Belle Vue, Morda Road. A photograph by John Maclardy. Belle Vue was renamed Glentworth in the mid-1880s.

Within the town of Oswestry, growth brought about by the arrival of the railways, and by the desire amongst those who could afford it to move from the increasingly crowded town centre to the edge of town, with its clean, healthier air, led to the development for the first time of enclaves of detached and semi-detached houses. These were typical Victorian villas, set in large, soon to be landscaped plots, to which the professional, technical and commercial classes could move. The 1891 Census shows that Queen's Road, at that time, was home to a solicitor, an auctioneer, a draper, an ironmonger, a retired farmer, a coal merchant, a boot merchant, a commercial traveller, a gunmaker, two ladies living on their own means, and a boys' boarding school run by John Evans M.A. The 1901 Census indicates that the residents of Morda Road included a solicitor, a schoolmaster, a brewer, a railway works manager, the superintendent to the Liverpool Corporation's aqueduct from Lake Vyrnwy, a retired chemist, a bootmaker's widow, a furniture dealer, a retired ironmonger, an assistant railway manager, a retired saddler, and a retired farmer from Berriew.

Houses in Morda Road, Oswestry. Photograph © John Pryce-Jones.

It was natural that these houses should be given names, rather than numbers – but what names would be chosen? For the most part, with a couple of exceptions, the names may strike us as rather bland, and unadventurous. In Morda Road, the row of houses built between the late 1880s and 1900, had names such as Ferndale, Longdendale, Gwynfynydd ('white mountain'), Abbotsford, Waverley, Croeswylan Villa, Glyndale, Dalesford, Bronderw ('oak ridge'), Knockfrink, Ebor House and Carreg Wylan ('weeping stone' reflecting the nearby Croeswylan Stone). By 1905, Longdendale had been renamed Glenhurst, the former name having been transferred to a house in Roft Street when the occupant moved there. Croeswylan Villa was renamed The Laurels, quite possibly to avoid confusion with the pre-existing detached house Croeswylan, also on Morda Road, built in the 1870s by the journalist and historian Askew Roberts. By 1910 Carreg Wylan was renamed Greengates, possibly for this same reason. Bronderw, meanwhile, had been renamed Rosneath by Charles Penrhyn Gasquoine, editor of the *Oswestry Advertizer*, to recall the name of his childhood home, built next to Croeswylan in the 1870s[80].

---

80  The original Rosneath had been renamed Wilmot Croft by the time of the 1881 Census

Whilst these latter details suggest that house names were in a state of permanent change, other evidence from Morda Road shows that this was not really the case: Ferndale, Abbotsford, Waverley, Glyndale, Ebor House and Dalesford remain unchanged to the present day; the name Gwynfynydd survived until 1940 after which date it was replaced by the present name Dunvegan; and Knockfrink remained in use until 1960 (changing to Eagle House at that time). Rosneath was renamed Rivendell, after Tolkein, in the late 1970s.

Turning to Queen's Road, the names follow a similar pattern. Houses on the estate were given names such as Orchard Croft, Craigielea, Normanhurst, Wynthorne, The Birches, Sherwood, Glenwood and Derwentdene; other houses, subsequently renamed, were initially given the names Sunnyside, Lynwood and Blythswood. As with Morda Road, these names may appear bland and a little disappointing, though in both cases it is without doubt deliberate that the names selected point to the sylvan, green and semi-rural location of these houses, emphasised by the use of terms such as wood, hurst, dale, dene and lea. The names also appear to have been chosen to provide a sense of solidity, of permanence, and of respectability. Many of the names do no more than that, but some do have other origins. Four have literary origins. The pair of semi-detached houses Abbotsford and Waverley in Morda Road suggest that their owner Adam Boyd, a native of Berwick on Tweed, who had moved to Oswestry in 1888 when he was appointed postmaster, was an enthusiast for the works of Sir Walter Scott. Ivanhoe, on the other side of Morda Road, was of course another of Scott's works; and Cranford at the junction of Queen's Road and Victoria Road, probably took its name from the novel of that name by Mrs Gaskell.

Of the 'sylvan' names, some did in fact have more specific origins. Craigielea was chosen by the boot merchant John Anderson to reflect his childhood home of Paisley, south-west of Glasgow, where there was a Craigielea House to the west of the town. Sherwood was chosen as a house name by Charles Denniss, general manager of the Cambrian Railways: it was his own middle name.

Houses in Queen's Road, Oswestry.  Photograph © John Pryce-Jones.

It is not clear why Rosneath, an area to the north of the Clyde estuary and the location of Rosneath Castle, Scottish home of the dukes of Argyll, was chosen by the Rev. Thomas Gasquoine for his Morda Road house.  However, for another Scottish name, Knockfrink, the Scottish genealogy website *scotlandspeople.gov.uk* has provided a straight forward explanation: the name was chosen by that house's first owner William Fraser, an officer of the Inland Revenue.  In the 1881 Census he was listed, then living in Park Avenue, Oswestry, as a native of Elgin, and use of the Scottish website enabled me first to locate his marriage, in Glasgow, in 1862, and then, using those details, his baptism, in 1832, the son of Alexander and Elspeth Fraser of Cnockfrink, on the burn of Advie in Speyside, in Elginshire.

Another house, on the opposite side of Morda Road, nowadays called Leeswood, had the name Friedenheim for a period of around ten years, until 1918.  The name is German for 'home of peace'.  The successor name Leeswood was chosen by Harold Whitfield Thomas whose parents had formerly lived at a house of that name, also on Morda Road, which by 1915 had been renamed Morda Lodge.

In concluding, it is worth noting that fieldwork alone – walking the streets with notebook and pencil - without reference to directories, census returns or electoral lists, can sometimes be misleading. In Oswestry's case, knowledge of the town's strong Welsh heritage might encourage the unwary to assume that the row of villas in Queen's Park now called Penlas ('green end'), Carreg Felin ('mill stone'), Llwyn ('grove'), Bronallt ('breast of the hill') and Hendre Wen ('white farmhouse') had long established names, each the choice of the original Welsh owners of these properties. In fact, none of these names dates back before 1950. As noted, these were respectively Breidden Cottage, Sunnyside, Lynwood, Oakley and Blythswood. Indeed, it is noteworthy how few of the houses in these two developments were given Welsh names when they were first built – in Queen's Park there was just one, Brynoswallt ('Oswald's hill'), soon changed to Rhianfa, perhaps to address possible confusion with the nearby Mount Oswald.

Secondly, and perhaps thankfully, whilst Dr Lewis commented in his lecture to the Centre for English Local History on the tendency in Sussex to use puns or other wordplay in choosing a name, this trait seems very largely absent in Oswestry, at least until more recent times. An interesting modern example of this tendency can be found on Morda Road, the name Elms Deep, given in the early 1970s to a new property built behind the substantial Victorian house whose original name had been Elmsdale (subsequently it was known as Dyffryn, and Valley Court). Clearly acknowledging the name Elmsdale, the name of course also alludes to Helm's Deep, from *Lord of the Rings*. It has already been noted that, also in the 1970s, Rosneath, on the opposite side of Morda Road, was renamed Rivandell. Why these Tolkein references? In part, they may reflect popular interest with *The Hobbit* and *The Lord of the Rings* trilogy in the late 1960s and 1970s, but it has been suggested to me that the reason might also relate to the location of these houses on Morda Road which, if mispronounced, either deliberately or otherwise, might bring to mind the name Mordor, the dwelling place of Sauron.

*Originally printed in the Salopian Recorder, the newsletter of the Friends of Shropshire Archives, for Summer 2014*

## Also by John Pryce-Jones

### Oswestry, a local history

Includes sixteen chapters, each describing a significant episode, character, or event in the history of Oswestry. Subjects include Old Oswestry hill fort, the railways, Edward Lhuyd, Napoleonic prisoners of war, the FitzAlans, and the annual Agricultural Show.

**ISBN 978 0 9517162 4 3**                                      **Price £4.95**

### Oswestry: parish, church and people

Includes eighteen chapters, each linked to Oswestry's ancient parish church. Topics range far and wide, from king Oswald to Victorian times, from the Civil War to the Indian Mutiny. *Oswestry: parish, church and people* gives readers a fascinating insight into past centuries, and parish life in Oswestry.

**ISBN 978 0 9517162 6 7**                                      **Price £3.95**

### An Oswestry miscellany

Includes twenty-five chapters, each focussed on a specific aspect of Oswestry's history, providing glimpses of the lives of past generations of Oswestrians. Topics range from the rumbustious election meeting addressed by David Lloyd George, to local football in the 1880s; from the capture of hedgehogs, to the laying out of the Broad Walk; from an outbreak of plague in Elizabethan times, to the shape of the church tower before the Civil War.

**ISBN 978 0 9517162 3 6**                                      **Price £4.95**

**Published by the Llanforda Press**